Thinking of...

Selling Microsoft Online Services?

Ask the Smart Questions

D1347794

By Frank Bennett and Dan Lewis

Smart Questions™ Philosophy

Smart Questions is built on 4 key pillars, which set it apart from other publishers:

1. *Smart people want Smart Questions not Dumb Answers*
2. *Domain experts are often excluded from authorship, so we are making writing a book simple and painless*
3. *The community has a great deal to contribute to enhance the content*
4. *We donate a percentage of revenue to a charity voted for by the authors and community. It is great marketing, but it is also the right thing to do*

www.Smart-Questions.com

Reviews

In this book Microsoft Online Services is mostly abbreviated to MS Online.

Although the Cloud might feel like hype right now, it's here to stay. Taking the Cloud seriously and changing the way you do business is something every business should consider. Thinking of…Selling Microsoft Online Services? is a great book which helps you understand which direction you should follow. Read it, make it your own and be successful in the Online Services world!

Danny Burlage, Founder and CTO, Wortell
www.wortell.nl

Thinking of…Selling Microsoft Online Services? is a straightforward, basic and quick read that positions the questions that need to be asked coupled with valuable answers that identify real world considerations. If you are thinking of selling MS Online, reading this book helps demystify and simplify the questions you might have around this game changing technology. I am glad I did!

Chris Teets, General Manager, Azaleos
www.azaleos.com

It would be easy to underestimate the impact that online services will have; easy but disastrous! If you think it's a threat you're probably right but doing nothing is an even bigger one - so read this book and start working out your way forward – the partners that figure out the best models earliest will be in great shape for the next 10 years.

Roger Collins, Managing Director, The CRM Business Ltd
www.thecrmbusiness.com

This book succinctly outlines the business opportunities around the Microsoft Online Services environment and shows how this can be highly rewarding. There's lots of new here and this book helps anyone thinking about an Online Services business understand what it's all about and helps you build a highly effective practice. Anyone in an IT business needs to read this now!

Nick Beaugeard, Managing Director, HubOne Pty Ltd
www.hubone.com

This book is of great value to all Microsoft partners interested in MS Online. It covers all the topics a business needs to address with clear, simple and, above all, useful suggestions to help guide the reader.

Richard Gibbons, Software Manager, Bechtle UK
www.bechtle.co.uk

As a Director of an IT Services Company I continually strive to keep abreast of industry solutions that could have a major effect on our business. The Cloud is a minefield of information and I need to be informed about new online services like MS Online and this book has enabled me to understand the enormity of MS Online as an offering. Furthermore it helped me to evaluate the overall impact MS Online will have on our and our clients' businesses and as a result we are now signed up as a partner to sell MS Online.

Samantha Hinton, Joint Managing Director, 81G Limited
www.81g.org

This book is essential reading for two reasons – market and customer requirements are changing rapidly and Microsoft has committed and invested in this opportunity. Microsoft's partners need to know how to embrace this change – it cannot be ignored. The new business models must be clearly understood, adapted and leveraged for each partner's own situation.

George Dziedzic, CEO, Foster MacCallum
www.foster-maccullum.com

As a Microsoft Large Account Reseller and SPLA* provider cloud computing is not new to us, but new initiatives from Microsoft like MS Online have allowed us to win new customers in new markets with a refreshing approach. Outsourcing allows clients to re-evaluate how software is purchased and reduces the costs of managing software. MS Online allows quicker adoption of new technologies and provides a new road for us into clients and new markets.

This book has provided food for thought and clearly guides a business through the steps when considering MS Online as a new business venture. Concise and informative.

Verity Affleck, SaaS Manager, PC-WARE
www.pc-ware.co.uk/saas

* SPLA (Service Provider Licence Agreement)

As with all emerging technology trends and solutions one of the first questions that must be answered is "How will this benefit my clients and does this make business sense for my company"? Online services such as MS Online is more than a trend; it's the beginning of an evolution of change to desktop and infrastructure services.

Reading this book helps a Microsoft partner determine what elements of online services make sense to their business model. It enables a partner to embrace a sound understanding of this evolution, helps you establish a foundation to deliver additional value to your clients, and positions you as providing thought leadership to assist clients with a long-term strategy to lower IT cost.

Lastly, this evolution is moving faster in today's economic climate, and a lower-cost cloud computing model will emerge faster with the introduction of online services.

David W. Hall, CTO, CompuCom Systems Inc.
www.compucom.com

Authors

Frank Bennett

Frank has a 30 year career in IT sales and marketing with large multi-national corporations and start-up early life companies. He has been involved in many evolutions of technology from mainframe computing through cloud computing. His insight of how the Internet is shaping commerce and customer buying behavior has helped many businesses define their go to market strategies.

Dan Lewis

Dan is a UK based IT trainer and consultant and has 15 years of industry experience with server operating systems and applications. He has trained administrators and end-users on a range of products including Windows Server, SharePoint and Exchange. He has presented at Microsoft TechNet events and delivered MS Online partner training courses on behalf of Microsoft in the UK and Ireland.

Table of Contents

Acknowledgements

The late British Prime Minister Harold Wilson was quoted as saying: "a week is a long time in politics". This book was first published in June 2009 prior to Microsoft WPC 2009 in New Orleans and if, as we do, you follow the reported news and events for Software as a Service and the Cloud it can also be said that "a week is a long time in IT".

There is a fever about change perhaps in part caused by the recent global recession and the desire to return to 'better times' but also driven by the IT industry looking for the next wave of growth.

We knew the time had come around to revise the book; Microsoft has the fever and is focusing its resources to build a world beating online services business. And had you noticed that the 'Cloud' is now common vocabulary for Microsoft?

In writing this book we have involved Sassan Saedi and his Microsoft Redmond based team and offer our thanks to them all (you know who you are) for reviewing the book and providing insight to MS Online developments.

To Stephen Parker and Ian Gotts architects of Smart Questions who helped with the ideas and structure for this book.

Foreword

Microsoft Online Services is enterprise-class software delivered as subscription services, hosted by Microsoft, and sold by our partners – and it is big business.

A shift is occurring and the world is abuzz with talk of the Cloud and how this presents new choices for customers to consume IT and Microsoft is Cloud ready with an inventory of products that create new wealth opportunities for our partners to grow their business.

This is a great time to go and talk to your customers and share ideas about how they can drive productivity in their businesses with MS Online. The world's most popular productivity applications are available as online services to include Exchange, SharePoint, Office Communications and Live Meeting under the Business Productivity Online Suite (BPOS) brand.

MS Online has broad appeal across small and large enterprises, as well as the public sector, and our partners play an important role in translating the benefits to customers and supporting them with a range of professional services.

This book, by Frank and Dan who themselves work in the Microsoft partner ecosystem, is written from a partner perspective. It highlights the MS Online market opportunity and how to earn money selling MS Online services. In June 2010 they published Thinking of...Selling Microsoft Online Services in Australia? Ask the Smart Questions. If you are an Australian reader then I invite you to contact Microsoft Australia for a copy of that book that has market specific information about the strategic alliance between Microsoft and Telstra for MS Online in that country.

Microsoft programs are in place to support our partners in selling MS Online and this book is timely in addressing the education needs of our partners who want to grow their business with Microsoft.

Sassan Saedi

Director, Online Partner Strategy, Microsoft Online Services

Microsoft Corporation

Who should read this book?

People like you and me

This book is not technical, nor was it ever intended to be. It is aimed squarely at those who see IT as a business and revel in the constant challenges of an industry that never ceases to innovate and amaze. For people who make decisions and advise others about strategy and business direction and choices that affect the future profits of a business this book is for you.

MS Online has broad appeal to small and large enterprises as well as the public sector and so presents many opportunities for Microsoft partners. For example:

- You are a business advisor/consultant and looking out for growth opportunities for your own business.

- You are a member of the Small Business Specialist Community (SBSC) [from October 2010 to be named 'Small Business' competency within the SMB category of the MPN[1]]. Your customers are particularly cost-conscious and looking for 'more for less' answers to their IT needs. Is MS Online part of that answer?

- You are a Medium Business Solution Provider and your customers want a partner that deeply understands their business process, infrastructure needs, and future growth costs. If your customers want to know more about how MS Online can meet their requirements are you ready to lead that discussion?

- You have public sector customers and their business decision making is often driven by policy and you will want to either be helping shape that policy or understand how the policy decisions affect your business conversations. We reveal a few surprises from the lips of public sector policy makers in the book.

---

[1] Microsoft Partner Network

- You have an installed base of customers with Microsoft products and are involved with their IT strategy and planning and you need to brief customers about MS Online – but not before you understand the implications for your business.

- You are a business owner and make decisions about investment that you make in IT to support the business. Is MS Online right for your business?

This book is intended to be a catalyst for action. Here are a few examples of the people who might be interested?

Owner, President, CEO

You have a responsibility to shareholders (that may be you), investors as well as employees to look into the future and make the right bets. You value your business relationship with Microsoft but may not fully understand the impact of the Cloud and in particular what MS Online means to your business. This book will help you work out the answers that you need to make the right decision for your business.

Your interest is financial

You may have heard that software licensing for software delivered over the Internet is different and impacts revenue and margins - it will. New subscription based pricing (pay as you go) needs to be assessed for its impact on cash flow. That is the financial impact and you will want to understand the market conditions that your sales and marketing team are wrestling with to compete for business. They have their own challenges too.

Your interest is technology

You know the Internet, Web 2.0, Azure and need to keep on top of the pressure the business puts on IT to deliver 'more usually for less'. The recession has put IT in the cross hairs of the finance team; we need savings what can you do this quarter to deliver 10%? You may have that pressure just as your customers do.

There has been a significant explosion of acronyms[2] recently; IaaS, PaaS, SaaS, and your customers' senior business executives read in the business pages about the Cloud as the 'fix' for IT.

---

[2] IaaS: Infrastructure as a Service, PaaS: Platform as a Service and SaaS: Software as a Service.

Along comes MS Online as a multi-tenant or dedicated tenant offer (more about these later) and you need to help your sales and marketing team understand the impact and how to proposition MS Online to customers among the other products and services you offer. What will be your strategy to support your sales team's customer conversations?

Your interest is sales

You want to maximize revenue and margin from every sale. Your sales team is increasingly facing customer conversations about the Cloud and their need to reduce costs. Do you wait for your customer to mention MS Online or do you take a proactive position and engage customers? The stakes are high.

Your interest is customer service

The reality is that the Cloud puts service at the heart of the customer relationship because the customer is paying a subscription with a renewal date that is their option to cancel, and a Partner of Record (PoR)[3] assignment they can change. The service they receive and their satisfaction is going to determine their decision. Service; easy to say and usually hard to do but increasingly recognized as a significant way to differentiate your business and earn customer loyalty.

How to use this book

This book is intended to be the catalyst for action. We hope that the ideas and examples inspire you to act. So, do whatever you need to do to make this book useful. Use Post-it notes and write on it. Rip it apart, or read it quickly in one sitting. Whatever works for you and we hope this becomes your most dog-eared book.

 This symbol is used throughout the book to draw your attention to an idea or something to consider – we hope that helps.

---

[3] Partner of Record (PoR) is terminology used by Microsoft to identify by name the partner nominated by a BPOS customer to. Microsoft pays fees to the PoR (details in Chapter 2) and the PoR should use this opportunity to deliver a range of professional services to BPOS customers as explained in Chapter 4.

Getting Involved

The Smart Questions community

There may be questions that we should have asked but didn't. Or specific questions which may be relevant to your situation, but not everyone in general. Go to the website *www.smart-questions.com* for the book and post the questions. You never know, they may make it into the next edition of the book. That is a key part of the Smart Questions philosophy.

Send us your feedback

We love feedback. We prefer great reviews, but we'll accept anything that helps take the ideas further. We welcome your comments on this book.

We'd prefer email, as it's easy to answer and saves trees. If the ideas worked for you, we'd love to hear your success stories. Maybe we could turn them into 'Talking Heads'-style video or audio interviews on our website, so others can learn from you. That's one of the reasons why we wrote this book. So talk to us.

feedback@Smart-Questions.com

Got a book you need to write?

Maybe you are a domain expert with knowledge locked up inside you. You'd love to share it and there are people out there desperate for your insights. But you don't think you are an author and don't know where to start. Making it easy for you to write a book is part of the Smart Questions Philosophy.

Let us know about your book idea, and let's see if we can help you get your name in print.

potentialauthor@Smart-Questions.com

Online is unstoppable

It is our choices...that show what we truly are, far more than our abilities.

J.K Rowling (Author of Harry Potter books)

Calling Microsoft partners

THE quotation may be an unusual choice as J.K Rowling is a fantasy author yet there is no fantasy about the Internet and its power and potential that has changed society. Did anyone really foresee the massive impact that the Internet would have on society and how we conduct business today?

 Everyday people go to work to figure out new ways to exploit the Internet and start-up businesses to develop their ideas and create products. If you stand still you get left behind real quick. There is no reason to get left behind when you are presented with an 'open door' from Microsoft to be a partner in the movement to online services[4] and the Cloud[5].

Microsoft is calling its partners to action to take MS Online to your customers.

---

[4] In this book 'Microsoft Online Services' abbreviated to 'MS Online' refers specifically to Microsoft's products whereas 'online services' is a general reference to online services/online service providers including Microsoft. Microsoft also use the term 'hosted services' and is used in this book.

[5] The Cloud is an abbreviation of Cloud Computing defined by Wikipedia as a style of computing in which dynamically scalable and often virtualized resources are provided as a service over the Internet.

MS Online comprises a number of products and in this book we make reference to Azure, Dynamics CRM, Windows Intune, Microsoft Office Web Apps and Business Productivity Online Suite (BPOS[6]). The focus of this book is to explain the opportunity for partners to sell BPOS while being mindful of the greater opportunity for partners to participate in the movement to MS Online. Jump to page 11 for a summary of the current products included in BPOS.

The world is ever-changing and while change can be viewed as a threat it also presents opportunity. We set out to explain this in more detail in the following chapters.

When we decided to write this book we were mindful of the needs of Microsoft partners to be able to quickly assimilate what is important and relevant to their business about MS Online and to earn money. The Cloud is new and for some difficult to explain (there are differing definitions, interpretations and opinions) and the word 'Cloud' is 'IT speak' and meaningless to most customers but MS Online is real and delivers meaningful benefits.

There is always a future to describe but if your need is to earn money today from offering your customers 'benefits' to their business then MS Online puts you in a great position to do that.

In this process it may throw up difficult questions and challenge assumptions about your future business plans but we are earnest in our purpose - to help you ask Smart Questions so you make the right decision for your business.

Microsoft taking the lead

The Cloud is in ascendancy with 1.8 billion Internet users (est. 2009[7]) and growing in number. This huge market is ripe with potential and that has attracted the interest of big business; IBM, Google, Cisco and Amazon (yes a bookstore!) to name a few. This is a here and now opportunity.

All analysts agree that Cloud is a high growth opportunity.

Your opportunity is to grab a share when you partner with Microsoft.

---

[6] BPOS: Business Productivity Online Suite a collection of Microsoft products for communication and collaboration delivered as a hosted service by Microsoft.

[7] Source *http://www.internetworldstats.com/stats.htm*

Many of the 1.8 billion Internet users already use Microsoft products so it is apparent that if Microsoft does not address this opportunity they put at risk the whole Microsoft community: shareholders, partners and customers. The opportunity and prize is too big to ignore so the situation defines itself – to do nothing is not an option for Microsoft.

Only by taking a lead role can Microsoft favorably shape and influence customers' buying decisions.

Does that make sense?

Microsoft is supporting you

The Microsoft partner eco-system is unrivalled in its size and geographical presence. The fact is, as a Microsoft partner, you rely on Microsoft for product innovation to fuel new business opportunities to earn money.

In today's markets troubled by economic turbulence, MS Online with its subscription pricing is ideally positioned for customers who want to deliver productivity in their business at a low monthly cost. MS Online addresses the business needs of your customers and positions you to serve the global appetite for online services[8].

Microsoft has positioned its partners to win with MS Online – are you ready?

MS Online is your deal

MS Online are enterprise-class software delivered as subscription services, hosted by Microsoft and sold by you – and it is big business.

In today's challenging market conditions your customers are ready to engage in conversation about how you can help them control costs and save money.

---

[8] Microsoft has an inventory of hosted 'online' assets, perhaps the best known being the free services of Hotmail and Live@edu. MS Online marks a change with propositions that partners can sell and deliver alongside their professional services to earn money.

Here are some potential scenarios:

Studies reveal 70% of your customers' annual IT costs are sunk in maintaining the IT they have already installed. The remaining 30% is spent on innovation; the new projects that they hope will deliver a source of increased productivity, differentiation and profit. In the current economic climate these innovation projects are not favored as they deliver returns in the future. Projects that deliver fast returns are in favor and are found by identifying costs savings in the current year that ideally recur.

IT is a significant cost to businesses and so it is subject to regular scrutiny. With the expanding availability of online services customers have further options on deciding economic choices to align IT costs with the financial outlook of the business.

To give an example; customers are looking at the comparative cost to run their own email service versus MS Online. No customer is going to switch off email to save money but what they are interested in is delivering email at the best value to the business and for some that will be with MS Online.

In many industries it is common to find that only information workers have access to computers and so it is the case that some workers have access to communication and collaboration tools and others do not.

Ask your customers; how do you communicate with the workers that do not have access to computers? They still need to communicate with them and so there is a cost to the business to do that; perhaps with letters sent to employees' homes or arranged meetings. Could these costs be better controlled and even reduced by providing these workers access to the same communication and collaboration tools used by other co-workers in the business?

Perhaps a reset in terms of how we approach conversations with customers is needed? For example: Mr. Customer, you can now run your email service implemented on-premises, as an online service or as a hybrid. Would you be interested to know: Which is the best value option while meeting all your operational needs?

 Is MS Online your opportunity to renew a conversation with customers that you have not had in a while?

Brighten you customer's day

There is nothing like some good news to lift your spirits, so here is the making of a good news story to brighten your customer's day.

In the wake of a global recession everything has come under hardened financial scrutiny including IT. With IT typically representing anything between 1 and 11% of sales (revenue) as a cost to a business it is a money conversation. Where your customers' sales have suffered during the recession this has put big pressure on them to deliver IT cost savings and that may have affected you as they delayed or cancelled IT spending plans. So that's the bad news. And the good news is?

A recent Microsoft survey[9] (published February 2010) among SMB customers revealed the most important reason a customer should consider the use of hosted services, like MS Online, in their business – *the impact on its financial performance.*

There is good news for your customers and you to act upon. We reveal this in the next chapter.

MS Online is evergreen

What would it be like to have an evergreen business?

Many businesses in the IT industry have recurring revenue streams from maintenance and other types of service contracts and it underpins the financial planning process and stability of the business through predictable cash flow.

MS Online presents an evergreen revenue opportunity and that is hugely appealing as a source of revenue that accumulates over time to deliver a Cumulative Monthly Recurring Revenue (CMRR) stream to the business.

Once you have read the book to understand the scope to earn money from the sale of MS Online then, as a suggestion, run some customer acquisition scenarios to see how that impacts the P&L over a one to five year period. You don't know what you don't know and scenario planning opens the mind to consider new possibilities. Better this way than to wonder or do nothing?

---

[9] *http://www.microsoft.com/presspass/press/2010/feb10/02-03TechCriticalPR.mspx*

Keep in mind that Microsoft has big ambitions for MS Online so BPOS is just one of many potential sources of revenue and margin.

You can start selling MS Online today or any time you are ready but keep in mind that the sooner you start the sooner you start to earn CMRR.

Your future – You decide

Microsoft will promote MS Online but the translation of this into business benefits for your customers is something that you are best positioned to do. In this book we look at this in more detail.

Our purpose is not to replicate the information that Microsoft make available online to partners. Rather we aim to help you make a business decision about selling MS Online and how to earn money.

The beauty and simplicity of MS Online with BPOS is that it enables business productivity through communication and collaboration and that is something every business[10] needs. MS Online provides a new approach to deliver productivity that will interest many customers and present opportunities for its partners (you) to earn money.

The opportunity is easy to access, easy to understand and to engage customers in conversation.

We now take you on a short as possible journey to your decision point to start earning money selling MS Online – after all, why keep your customers waiting?

---

[10] In this book references to business and businesses is inclusive of for profit, not-for-profit and the public sector (government) who all use the term 'business' when describing their purpose, as in; in our business….

But it is your decision

 You could let your customers figure out what MS Online means for their business and leave it to them to make their own buying decisions and maybe go talk to other suppliers

OR

 Choose to take the lead and advise your customers how they use MS Online as part of the solution to grow their businesses and manage their costs.

This is no time to bury you head in the sand - it is decision time.

Chapter 2

Microsoft raise online stakes

Ability will never catch up with the demand for it.

Malcolm Forbes *(US art collector, author, & publisher, 1919 - 1990)*

MICROSOFT has a significant and growing inventory of online services and MS Online presents partners the opportunity to earn money from fees and professional services – so the stakes are raised for partners to participate in this growth business.

As a Microsoft partner you will have honed your skills to sell, deliver and support the on-premises installation of hardware and software.   It may be your reaction to treat online services as a threat? In reality online services is an opportunity - the threat is ignoring them. The reason being; online services present the opportunity to *sell more to more customers* so if you ignore it then your business misses out on this opportunity.

Consider for one moment; could online services be your chance to win customers with an innovative solution and the opportunity to offer your professional services?

Things are changing for Microsoft with MS Online and for its partners. Now we look at, in three parts, the things that are new and different about selling MS Online and how you can earn money delivering a breadth of professional services.

BPOS – Part 1

In this Part 1 we look at the business topics as they affect your interest to sell MS Online as a Microsoft Advisor[11].

BPOS is a major investment in online services and in your future

Microsoft has invested in multiple data centers around the world in recognition of the geo-political nature of the Cloud[12]. It is lobbying legislators to agree appropriate rules and where required laws for data privacy and protection and to ensure that these are conducive to the many benefits of Cloud. Make no mistake that Microsoft is chasing down this opportunity with all its corporate muscle and fervor.

The extent of Microsoft's investment in its datacenters is not public information but it is reported to be billions of dollars – this is big business. You can be part of it.

As Microsoft hosts the MS Online service the cost and complexity of hosting is removed and by doing this on a global scale they achieve economies of scale that would not otherwise be possible.

This is your opportunity to participate in selling BPOS to your customers backed by the trusted reputation of Microsoft.

 This is as easy as it gets to start earning money selling online services with BPOS – you've been given the keys to the car if you want to drive it?

So, what is BPOS?

BPOS offers partners a new business opportunity to sell online services and generate revenue from fees earned as the Partner of Record and from professional services[13] sold to existing and new

---

[11] You can enrol as a Microsoft Advisor through the Microsoft Partner Network web site. The URL is provided in the Appendix – Online Resources.

[12] More details can be found at *http://www.globalfoundationservices.com*

[13] Because the word services is used many times in this document (e.g. hosted services) to avoid confusion we have used "professional services" to describe the paid for services (customisation, integration, migration, development, support, your expertise) sold by a partner (you) to a BPOS customer. Your professional services are a key factor in your success with MS Online services as will be described later.

customers. In today's tough economic conditions this may be music to your ears?

BPOS makes available a number of products as a hosted solution sold individually or as a suite with the solutions hosted by Microsoft in their own data centers and sold by Microsoft Advisors.

Customers looking for solutions to improve productivity will be interested in BPOS. The current products available are:

- Microsoft Exchange Online (incl. Forefront for Exchange)
- Microsoft SharePoint Online
- Microsoft Office Live Meeting
- Microsoft Office Communications Online
- Microsoft Exchange Online Deskless Worker
- Microsoft SharePoint Online Deskless Worker
- Microsoft SharePoint Online Extra Storage
- Blackberry support[14]

All products are currently Microsoft's 2007 version. These will be updated to the 2010 versions; however timing for this is not yet fixed. Keep watching your favorite MS Online news source for details (see the suggested links in the Appendix).

BPOS Service types

To meet the needs of a broad spectrum of customers BPOS is available in two service types: multi-tenant and dedicated tenant. The simplest way to position the service type with customers is by reference to the user numbers.

Standard BPOS (BPOS-S) offering is multi-tenant (shared instance) and is the standard for most customers with user numbers in the range 1 to 20,000 (although it can scale to 30,000+ seats).

---

[14] Blackberry App Version 4.5 or higher

Dedicated tenant (BPOS-D) is typically targeted at the Enterprise customer with 5000 or more seats, although it is economically suited to higher seat counts (typically over 20,000).

More to come

Microsoft aim to greatly expand their portfolio of cloud based services over the coming years and BPOS with its communication and collaboration capabilities will be a core service so expect on-going enhancements.

A number of additional management options and user features have been added over the last 18 months including much enhanced migration tools. At the same time storage limits have increased dramatically and the pricing has been reduced post-launch (timely as customers wrestle with costs in the wake of a global recession).

The MS Online service is set for a major upgrade to the 2010 versions of the relevant server products. Microsoft has still not fixed the timing for this, although it is likely to be early in 2011. This will ensure customers have access to the latest version of the software as that available for deployment on-premises.

Progress without the pain

What makes BPOS different from many other hosted offerings is Microsoft's commitment to provide integration with your customers' existing investments in Microsoft server and desktop software. This is not only important for customers but also preserves a partner's investment in training and skills.

All you need to access BPOS is a browser. However many customers may want to, or need to, enhance the user experience with the addition of client and server software.

 Software-plus-Services: all the benefits of a hosted service combined with the power and functionality of client and server software.

Power of Choice

One of the golden rules of selling taught at sales school – *offer your customer a choice.*

This has taken on a new significance with the availability of online services from Microsoft.

No customer can afford the option to throw away perfectly sound investments in IT that are installed on customer's premises (on-premises) and work. However, it is true that customers, and this is particularly so during the impact and aftershock of the global recession, have had to look at costs in the business and IT has come under the microscope.

This has resulted in a slowdown in customer IT spending with a focus on maintaining rather than renewing and innovating as well as a review of headcount. We believe this has sharpened the mind of business to look at IT with a hardened financial 'hat-on'[15].

The widespread publicity of SaaS, Cloud and online services and its booming availability has brought this to the attention of customers who now want to know 'what it means' for their business. Who will they turn to for that help and advice? If that is the case what might be the context of your next customer conversation?

Will you take the lead in that conversation or will your customer?

Later in this chapter and in chapter 4 we look at some actions that you can take in preparation to lead the conversation with you customers.

IT Transformation – driven by need to reduce costs and 'look at alternatives'

Legacy IT
Own and Operate
Build to Order

CAPEX and people intensive

SaaS / On Demand
Configure to Order
Services Culture

OPEX and collaborative with partners

If as remarked, businesses are not about to 'throw away', then a starting place would be to talk to whoever sold and/or maintains their existing IT assets. You perhaps?

A customer's management team conversation might go along the lines of: "What can we do to preserve and extend the useful

---

[15] The language of Capex and Opex and its relevance to a customer's decision making is elevated with the availability of online services like MS Online that is treated as Opex.

working life (the use of 'extend' is deliberate and pertinent to the economic situation) of our current IT investment (it works and staff are trained to use it) and take advantage of the economics of SaaS and the Cloud in our business?"

Your sales team conversation: "Why might MS Online be important to our customers? And, how, if we decide to, can we introduce a conversation with our customers about MS Online and demonstrate value so they start spending with us?"

And the conversation you take as a partner to your customers? There's a story.

What really matters to your customer?

- They need IT and it is a cost they absorb but how much do you know about the cost of IT to your customers' business?
- Do you know the cost of IT as a percentage of your customers' sales revenue or income if they are not-for-profit organizations or in the public sector?
- Does your customer benchmark their IT costs against their competitors or peers?
- Or is that something that you should do?

The UK budget airline EasyJet is priced for the cost-conscious traveler so every penny counts in keeping costs low to deliver the attractive fares that put passengers on their aircraft seats. They don't have the luxury to be extravagant on IT spending and measure their IT costs as a percentage of revenue, yet IT plays a vital role in the day to day operation of the airline and keeping aircraft on schedule. The target for IT is to deliver 100% availability; but at what price?

The answer: see footnote[16].

Businesses everywhere, in the wake of the recession are looking to repair their balance sheets and re-build their cash reserves and perhaps are more open than ever before to re-evaluate options.

Just as you tend to do when you have a shock in your personal life.

---

[16] At a Microsoft UK partner event (May 2010) it was told by an EasyJet employee their IT costs are 0.75% of EasyJet's sales revenue.

Plan the dive and dive the plan

A lesson taught to divers and also a discipline 'for getting things done'.

How might you start to engage in a conversation with your customers that builds a constructive dialogue to jump start spending on IT in the business?

Do your customers jump at the unsolicited proposal to upgrade to Exchange 2010 or do they crave a different discussion?

For example: What is the optimal allocation of cost to deliver IT to the business?

A map of that discussion would have the key IT systems that a customer uses categorized as below:

EXAMPLES	IMPORTANCE	AVAILABILITY
Core Business Applications (make us better/different)	Vital to 'what we do' and intolerant to downtime	Target 100%
Non-Differentiating Applications (we have them and so do others)	Help us get the job done; email is in this category	Expectation is 100%

For the most part these applications have been implemented on-premises because there was not a viable alternative – until now.

The power of choice is now available to you to assist your customers to look at the economics and best way to deliver on availability for their applications. In some cases that may mean no change and they remain on-premises. Others may be better suited for delivery as an online service.

 Customers are interested in progress but not at any price and opening up a discussion about choices is a friendly way to develop ideas and customer enthusiasm.

BPOS market availability

BPOS is currently available in 39[17] countries. If you have customers with multi-country locations then consider the availability of BPOS to serve the diverse needs of their business (HQ, remote office, project office, home workers, mobile workers) and the language[18] requirements.

MS Online "in-market" actors

Microsoft

Host MS Online services as they do for all MS Online customers worldwide.

Partners

Register as a Microsoft Advisor within the Microsoft Partner Network to sell MS Online and be eligible to be a PoR. See Appendix – Online Resources for URL.

Customer

MS Online customers contract for the service(s) with Microsoft and decide who will be their Partner of Record.

 Note that customers with Enterprise Agreements for Microsoft products can engage directly with Microsoft or their LAR[19] for the provision of MS Online offerings.

---

[17] Here is the alphabetical list of the 39 countries where BPOS-S (Standard) offering is available: Australia, Austria, Belgium, Brazil, Canada, Costa Rica, Chile, Colombia, Czech Republic, Cyprus, Denmark, Finland, France, Germany, Greece, Hong Kong, Hungary, India, Ireland, Italy, Israel, Japan, Luxembourg, Mexico, Netherlands, New Zealand, Norway, Peru, Poland, Portugal, Puerto Rico, Romania, Singapore, Spain, Sweden, Switzerland, Trinidad & Tobago, UK and United States.

[18] Microsoft states that the products that comprise BPOS are localized in up to 45 languages; and the Microsoft Online Customer Portal is localized in 18 different languages. Check with Microsoft for the latest information related to supported languages.

[19] Large Account Reseller

BPOS – Part 2

In this Part 2 we look at the partner program aspects of MS Online including pricing. The partner program is expansive and we list here those aspects with language that you may yet to become familiar with:

Partner of Record

Customer Portal

Try before you Buy

Service Level Agreement

Commerce Dashboard

Delegated Administration

Internal Use Rights

Demo Account

Partner of Record

Customers enter into a contract with Microsoft and make payment directly to Microsoft for the MS Online services they subscribe to.

A customer names a Partner of Record (PoR) who will typically (but not always) provide professional services including end user support to the customer and be the party to receive PoR fees from Microsoft.

This means there is no commercial transaction between the PoR and the customer for the subscription fees for the MS Online service(s). As the PoR named by the MS Online customer you will receive fees paid to you by Microsoft all the time the customer remains under contract and you remain the PoR.

At the time of writing:

- Partners earn a 12% referral fee based on the initial 12 month contract value for all net-add[20] acquisitions.

---

[20] Net-add is Microsoft terminology for new license sales whether to a new customer or an existing customer adding additional licenses.

- Partners earn 6% ongoing as recurring fees, as long as the customer's subscription remains active and you are the designated PoR. This gives a year 1 total of 18%.

- Partners will also be paid fees based on any additional seats that a customer buys at a later stage (both the 12% net-add and 6% recurring fees are paid).

The payment of the fees to the PoR by Microsoft is made on a quarterly basis.

Pricing for BPOS

Customers are attracted to hosted services with subscription pricing keeping start-up costs low and on-going costs predictable and affordable.

A customer can purchase individual BPOS products but benefit from a lower price when buying the suite of products compared with the sum of the individual components and that is a 'deal' and driver for increasing the professional services that you offer.

Microsoft Exchange Online	US$5.00/month
Microsoft SharePoint Online	US$5.25/month
Microsoft Office Live Meeting	US$4.50/month
Microsoft Office Communications Online	US$2.00/month
Microsoft Business Online Productivity Suite comprising all four products above	US$10.00/month
Microsoft Exchange Online Deskless Worker	US$2.00/month
Microsoft Online SharePoint Deskless Worker	US$2.00/month
Microsoft Deskless Worker Suite comprising the two products above	US$3.00/month

Pricing is per license (aka seat or user) applicable at time of publication of this book (June 2010). For detailed and current pricing for all BPOS components please refer to
http://www.microsoft.com/online/buy.mspx#guide.

BPOS has a 5 user minimum for the initial order and a minimum contract term of 12 months that is evergreen. There is no minimum for additional users for the same service.

Price discounts are available for volume orders and are determined for each individual service subscription (not an aggregate of all service subscriptions). The table below relates order volume to price levels that determine the actual pricing when added to the shopping cart at *https://mocp.microsoftonline.com/*

Quantity	Price Level
5 to 249	1
250 to 2,399	2
2,400 to 5,999	3
6,000 to 14,999	4
15,000 and above	5

Licenses are currently available to purchase in these 11 currencies: Australian Dollar - British Pound - Canadian Dollar - Danish Krone – Euro - Japanese Yen - New Zealand Dollar - Norwegian Kroner -Swedish Krona - Swiss Franc - U.S. Dollar.

Calculation of PoR fees

Example calculation of PoR fees based on US$ pricing:

Customer purchases 20 user BPOS suite annual price $2,400.00 (20x$10x12)

- PoR earns $288 in Year 1 in net-add initial fees (12% of $2,400.00)

- PoR earns $144 in recurring fees (6% of $2,400.00) in Year 1 and each year thereafter to the PoR while the customer remains under contract

- In Year 1 PoR earns in total $432.00

- In each year thereafter PoR earns $144.00

 The fees paid by Microsoft to a PoR are one part of the total revenue and margin to be earned from the sale of BPOS. Your upside opportunity is in professional services.

BPOS has a Customer Portal

The Microsoft Online Services Customer Portal (MOCP) is where customers go to sign up for a trail of BPOS and to make purchases.

The essential functions of the MOCP support:

- The creation of a profile for the service(s)

- The activation of a trial of a service(s) and purchases

- Selection of a Partner of Record (PoR)

- Management of subscriptions

The URL for the MOCP can be found in the Appendix.

As a partner you can initiate a trial of BPOS for a customer, generate and send a quotation for BPOS services to a customer for purchases and this is covered in the next Chapter.

MS Online licensing

The MS Online products currently available include:

Online Service name	*Available now*
Microsoft Exchange Online (including Forefront for Exchange)	√
Microsoft SharePoint Online	√
Microsoft Office Live Meeting	√
Microsoft Office Communications Online	√
Microsoft Business Productivity Online Suite (BPOS)	√
Blackberry Support	√
Microsoft Exchange Online Deskless Worker*	√
Microsoft SharePoint Online Deskless Worker*	√
Microsoft SharePoint Online Extra Storage	√
Microsoft Dynamics CRM Online	*Currently USA, Canada and Puerto Rico only***

* available as individual MS Online service or as a suite known as the Online Deskless Worker Suite.

** - recent anouncements indicate that this will expand in 2H2010 -
http://www.microsoft.com/presspass/press/2010/apr10/04-25convergencecrmpr.mspx

Check with Microsoft Licensing for other licensing terms (e.g. Enterprise Agreement (EA)) and latest promotions.

Customers offered Try before you Buy

Microsoft currently offers customers a 20 user license, 30 day free trial of the BPOS Suite and BPOS Deskless Worker Suite.

Customers like try before you buy and can proceed with a trial on their own so it wise to consider how you engage with your customers now BPOS is available. Try not to let that happen when there is a better way as described here.

It is important to understand your customer's current business needs and how BPOS can answer those needs. This is the foundation for qualification of a potential sale and may be sufficient to close the sale but if it is not then consider one of the following options:

1. Run a demonstration for your customer using the demo account available to partners.
2. Move your customer into a trail with the customer in self service mode with an agreement to a review on day 10, day 20 and day 30 of the trial by setting calendar invites to attend a Live Meeting.
3. Move your customer to make a purchase (they can cancel within 30 days) and manage the trial. The trail must address known business requirements and engage the people that will be users as the user experience will be an important factor in the decision.
4. Your customer may have particular requirements that require customization, for example of SharePoint, and you proceed as in 2. above with a proof of concept where your professional services are paid for or on contingence – you decide.

 It is important your customers' name you as their PoR so you earn fees payable to a PoR. Can you assume that will happen if you are not involved in their trial?

If you engage your customers in a trial it is important that you remain in contact during the 30 day trial period to learn about their experience, provide guidance and of course ensure that you are confirmed as the PoR when they purchase.

Service Level Agreement (SLA)

It is customary for hosted service providers to provide a SLA and one important aspect of that relates to availability of the service. Microsoft understands the importance that customers attach to a SLA and target 99.9% availability in any month and will financially compensate customers if they fail to deliver (conditions as always apply: the SLA customer documents are available online to download at www.microsoft.com).

Where the availability is <99.9% Microsoft pay back to customer a proportion of the monthly fee payable by customer.

If the availability is <95% Microsoft pay back to customer the full monthly fee payable by customer.

 Compare this to on-premises installations where a failure usually results in a customer incurring additional costs. You can see how compelling this is to customers?

MS Online Partner Sales Portal

The MS Online Partner Sales Portal assists a partner to promote and sell BPOS. To access the Sales Portal go to the Microsoft Online Service Partner Sales Portal and sign in with your Windows Live ID.

Once signed in to the Sales Portal a partner can perform certain activities proactively for a customer; for example, initiate a trial of BPOS or raise a quotation for BPOS.

The significance of the Partner Sales Portal is to put a partner (you) in a position to promote and sell BPOS to customers and assert your role as the PoR.

Using the Sales Portal a partner can initiate a trial for a customer by sending an email to customers and prospects with a URL to follow to complete the registration process and commence a trial of BPOS. To set up a trial requires 10 fields of information, 4 of which will be pre-populated by the partner to include the partner as PoR, and so by taking a proactive stance you simplify the activation process for a customer to start a trial and lay claim to being the PoR.

As an alternative to sending a URL out via email you could run campaigns via a marketing web site with a URL for a customer to click through and commence a trial or make a purchase. As and when Microsoft have pricing offers on subscriptions to BPOS additional links could be added for the duration of that offer. When a customer is ready to buy the partner can raise a quotation and send that to the customer for authorization. Only the customer can authorize the purchase but the partner is involved in the transaction and importantly gets to insert their name as PoR when preparing the quotation.

This outreach can be customized for sales people for sales campaign and commission tracking purposes.

In summary, the Partner Sales Portal helps a partner engage a customer in a trial leading to a purchase or outright purchase with no trial of BPOS.

 Use the Partner Sales Portal as a sales tool to promote BPOS and win business and establish your position as the customer's PoR.

Commerce Dashboard

The dashboard provides a partner with a view of all their BPOS transactions. For example:

- There are reports which provide information on which of your customers trials or paid contracts are due to expire that will signal you to proactively discuss purchases, renewals and modifications to the services.
- It provides various statistics on trial to paid conversions and year on year renewals.
- A record of those BPOS customers that you are named as PoR to include the PoR fees earned as well as fully detailing payments made or due on a customer by customer basis (handy for forecasting).
- Sales people can track their customers; each quote made from the Partner Sales Portal is given a unique ID and can be tracked in the Commerce Dashboard.

Delegated Administration

Where a PoR is granted Delegated Administration they are active in the administration of a customer's BPOS service and in doing so earn money. A customer can grant and rescind Delegated Administration to a PoR.

One of the benefits to partners of the Delegated Administration feature is that it provides a single view that simplifies the administration of multiple BPOS customers, eliminating the need to log into individual customer's BPOS portals.

Partners that are familiar with providing managed services will relish this opportunity and even if you are not offering managed services this is your opportunity to do so.

Partners must be eligible to granted Delegated Administration and are referred to as Accelerated Partners.

 Consider the impact of the recurring revenue opportunities from managed services combined with PoR fees earned to grow your business.

Where you are actively involved in the management of BPOS for a customer with Delegated Administration then you are much higher in the value chain with detailed knowledge of how BPOS is used by your customer - that is a privileged position.

As the table reveals there is commonality between the professional services that you already provide to customers on-premises with those that are needed by customers using Online Services. This means that all your existing skills are transferrable to Online Services.

For those activities that Microsoft performs you would typically be the first point of contact for your customer and you would escalate the request to Microsoft as appropriate. For example, if your customer reported to you that certain email items were corrupted you would collect as much information about the lost items as possible and then initiate a service request from within the BPOS administration portal. It is worth noting that some activities relating to recovery of accidentally deleted content are chargeable by Microsoft.

This is only the beginning as Online Services expand over time with new functionality and additional products your investment in BPOS is the foundation for growing your business with Microsoft Online Services.

Partner Internal Use Rights

A partner that has signed up to sell BPOS is offered up to 250 seats to run in their own business (internal use rights only) for a period of one year. To maintain this free benefit in subsequent years a partner will need to achieve defined sales targets (these are currently being determined by Microsoft).

Partner Demo Account

To help partners learn about the features and benefits of BPOS a 20 seat demo account is offered.

Both these benefits, IUR and demo account, provide partners an ideal way to learn about BPOS by using it themselves and to create full feature demonstrations to assist with the sales process. For example; using the Live Meeting service to demonstrate BPOS helps the customer to visualize the potential of BPOS and to see how they might use Live Meeting in their business.

BPOS – Part 3

In this Part 3 we look at the product related aspects of BPOS.

BPOS is rich in functionality

You will likely be familiar with some or all of these products described below and want to understand the implications of them being available to your customers as a hosted solution. A short description for each of these follows.

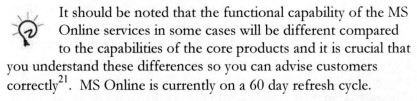 It should be noted that the functional capability of the MS Online services in some cases will be different compared to the capabilities of the core products and it is crucial that you understand these differences so you can advise customers correctly[21]. MS Online is currently on a 60 day refresh cycle.

This creates an opportunity for you to consider your customers' requirements to understand and advise the appropriate solution delivered as MS Online, on-premise, partner hosted or a combination.

 Microsoft Advisor is more than just a random choice of name.

Microsoft Exchange Online delivers e-mail services including spam filtering, anti-virus protection, and synchronization with mobile devices. Through Microsoft Office Outlook 2007[22] and Microsoft Office Outlook Web Access, you can use the advanced

---

[21] Available from Microsoft Download Centre at www.microsoft.com

[22] Neither the Outlook or Entourage clients are included in the MS Online pricing

e-mail, calendar, contact, and task management features of Exchange Online. Office Outlook Web Access enables users to access their e-mail messages from almost any browser—whether the user is in the office or out on the road. Macintosh users are supported by Microsoft's Entourage email client software.

Microsoft SharePoint Online allows customers to share and work together on documents, maintain version control for shared documents, create intranet sites to manage projects and project workflows, post calendar information, and set up wikis and blogs.

Microsoft Office Live Meeting allows online meetings with colleagues, customers, and partners in real time. Office Live Meeting participants can convene online to share documents, ask questions, work on a virtual "whiteboard" and talk to each other during the meeting.

Microsoft Office Communications Online delivers robust instant messaging (IM) and presence functionality that enables real-time person-to-person communication via text, voice and video, across an organization.

Microsoft Exchange Online Deskless Worker and Microsoft SharePoint Online Deskless Worker

Also available as the Online Deskless Worker Suite (both products) and provide some of the features of Exchange Online and SharePoint Online to workers that are not desk bound, for example those in customer service and retail. Be sure to check the features supported and qualify against your customer's requirements. For example; Exchange Online Deskless Worker does not provide mobility access and SharePoint Online Deskless Worker does not allow a user to create, edit and save documents. Many workers today do not have access to the messaging and collaboration tools used by other co-workers and that is now addressed with these products.

Microsoft is hard at work

Microsoft aim to greatly expand their portfolio of cloud based services over the coming years and BPOS for its communication and collaboration capabilities will be a core service so expect on-going enhancements.

A number of additional management options and user features have been added over the last 18 months including much enhanced migration tools. At the same time storage limits have increased and the pricing has been reduced (timely as customers wrestle with costs in the wake of a global recession).

The MS Online service is set for a major upgrade to the 2010 versions of the relevant server products. Microsoft has still not fixed the timing for this, although it is likely to be early in 2011. This will ensure customers have access to the latest version of the software as that available for deployment on-premises. There is currently a lag between the availability of a software release of the on-premise server versions and the upgrade of the online service to that release. But bear in mind, customers don't have the strain of implementation or any cost associated with upgrades to the online service as this is all provided for in the subscription to MS Online services - future-proofed for customers.

With the incremental changes and scheduled major upgrades to MS Online services it is important to handle your customer expectations. Although for most customers it will be an advantage to always have access to the latest version of the service, others may want to consider the impact on the user experience as it might affect productivity of their employees. At the same time you will need to keep on top of your game so not to be caught out by modifications and enhancements to the management interfaces and tools.

Online and Software-plus-Services

What makes BPOS different from many other hosted offerings is Microsoft's commitment to provide integration with your customers' existing investments in Microsoft server and desktop software. This is not only important to customers but also preserves your investment in training and skills and creates professional services opportunities.

All you need to access BPOS is a browser. However many customers may want to, or need to, enhance the user experience with the addition of client and server software.

Here are some examples:

- Outlook 2007 is the client for both Exchange Online and SharePoint Online and provides caching and an offline working mode when working without an internet connection.

- Word, Excel and PowerPoint 2007 can both be used to open and save documents directly to SharePoint Online to give users a very similar experience to working with a traditional file system.

- Access 2007 contains wizards that assist with the migration of databases to SharePoint based applications.

- InfoPath 2007 can be used to create professional looking forms which can be stored and accessed from SharePoint.

- Communicator 2007 is the client for Communications Online and provides instant messaging and user presence information.

- SharePoint Designer 2007 is free and used to customize the look and feel of SharePoint and also to create workflow based business applications. It can also be used to create backups of content and allow for imports and exports of files and configurations.

- Live Meeting 2007 Client is free and provides the best experience of Live Meeting including full data, audio (VOIP) and video sharing and meeting management.

- The BPOS sign-in tool (free with BPOS) simplifies the logon experience by automatically authenticating the user to all the BPOS services without them being prompted for a user name and password. This ensures that the online experience is like that to access an on-premises server deployment of applications.

- The Active Directory synchronization tool (free with BPOS) keeps a customer's local Active Directory synchronized with BPOS and can be used as part of a migration along with the mailbox migration tool.

 Software-plus-Services: all the benefits of a hosted service combined with the power and functionality of client and server software.

More of what you already do

MS Online raises the stakes for customers and for partners with the choices to deploy software on-premises, partner hosted, Microsoft hosted or a combination of these.

 Your professional services opportunity expands with online services and you may regard this as an important point of differentiation for your business.

You will be interested to know how you monetize this opportunity and we cover that in Chapter 4.

Be Online Smart

None of us is as smart as all of us.

Philip Murray Condit an American *businessman and* Chairman *and CEO of the* Boeing *Company from 1996 to 2003.*

S O that you are ready for the conversation with your customers we reference below recent Microsoft developments that shape those conversations.

"We're all in"

Steve Ballmer CEO of Microsoft Corporation said: "We are all in"; as he talked about Microsoft's commitment to the Cloud.

If you are a Microsoft partner recognize that Microsoft is focusing its massive resources on the Cloud and that is a big 'think about it' declaration from the world's largest software company.

So, what else is in store?

Azure

Azure is a Cloud based offering from Microsoft. Whereas BPOS provides specific Microsoft services (e.g. SharePoint Online), Azure is 'open' to support developers to deploy their applications and services in the Cloud. A simple way of thinking of Azure is a Windows Server platform running in the Cloud as a service to run applications on. Given the nature of the Cloud to provide dynamically allocated elastic compute and storage resources this is a big opportunity to work with your customers to optimally configure computing resources for their business scenarios.

Here are some examples of business scenarios that are suited to the use of Cloud services like Azure and MS Online services:

Start-Up business

Cash is in short supply and the IT capacity needs of the new business are largely unknown but need to be available as the business grows. Many Venture Capitalist firms that are providing funding for start-up businesses are insisting the business use the Cloud to free up cash for R&D and sales and marketing rather than spent on IT assets. They also recognize that if the business succeeds it needs to scale fast and the Cloud makes that easy.

On/Off business

Some businesses have on/off requirements for IT capacity. If you are planning to run a 4 week marketing campaign starting in 2 weeks time then you have a need to; switch on (start costs), then switch off (stop costs). This scenario also entails the need to cope with unpredictable demand.

Unpredictable demand

IT capacity is generally matched to the normal operating requirements of a business to avoid the burden (cost) of too much capacity that is underutilized. A business only needs to add capacity when it is needed and sometimes that is hard to predict so the Cloud is ideally suited to this situation.

Predictable demand

Many businesses have cyclical trading periods that result in heavy IT loads at a trading end period or accounting end period. In the retail industry December and January are big trading months. In the IT industry the last few days before a year-end can be frantic for order processing, inventory, logistics, invoicing and accounts receivable. The peak workload is predictable but providing the compute and storage capacity for these periods results in under-utilization at other times. With the Cloud the resources can be dynamically allocated on-demand. Problem solved.

Azure – for the practical minded

This is a heads up on Azure if you need the full monty[23] then you need to read another Smart Questions title[24].

Azure is made up of three components

- Windows Azure provides the platform and if required the Internet Information Server (IIS) and .NET components
- SQL Azure provides a highly available and high performance data storage system
- The Azure AppFabric is the glue that binds the applications, operating system and database engine together allowing the customer to create flexible Cloud solutions

Applications can be written in a variety of languages to work on Azure. Pricing is based upon transactions, storage space and computational power consumed rather than user licenses.

Your customers may be interested in migrating in-house applications to Azure to achieve lower costs than can be achieved with on-premises compute and storage resources. They may be looking at new applications, a new web service or web site for their partners or customers, and want to compare the economics of deployment in the Cloud versus on-premises.

Now you can advise your customers how to deploy IT in 3 ways: online services with MS Online, on-premises and partner hosted.

Change + Innovation + Action = Opportunity.

When? Now, just as soon as you are ready!

Tools for IT

Managing IT is an activity that keeps businesses and IT departments (if they have them) very busy (and stressed). This presents an opportunity for managed service providers.

With IT potentially distributed on-premises, partner hosted, as an MS Online service and deployed with Azure the management task is changing and Microsoft is addressing this new fabric of online

---

[23] Meaning the complete, whole thing

[24] Delivering Solutions on the Windows Azure Platform ISBN 978-0-9561556-3-4

service management. Microsoft is in the process of transitioning a number of their System Centre IT Infrastructure management products to the Cloud.

One of the first examples is Windows Intune (available as a beta in North America); an online service for managing, monitoring and securing Windows PCs over the internet. It also provides hardware and software inventory tracking, can enable software updates and allows for remote control of a PC from any location. Windows Intune can be used by any organization but is ideal for mobile workforces that cannot easily schedule time to hand over their PC to their IT department or service provider to troubleshoot or update.

New and coming soon

Psst! Microsoft Office Web Apps 2010.

One of the major changes to BPOS which is due 2011 is the addition of Office Web Apps 2010 which will allow for access and editing of Word, Excel, PowerPoint and OneNote documents via a supported browser[25] with no other software requirement on the local device.

There will be integration into Outlook Web App and SharePoint to allow direct working with any documents stored in emails as attachments or document libraries. The addition of Office Web Apps provides an important piece of the jigsaw to allow user mobility and device independence.

It is also worth noting that advertising supported versions of these applications are being provided to anyone with a Microsoft Live ID via Hotmail and SkyDrive.

---

[25] As of May 2010 Microsoft support Internet Explorer 7 or later for Windows, Safari 4 or later for Mac, and Firefox 3.5 or later for Windows Mac or Linux

The expanding world

Earlier in the book we stated there are c.1.8Bn Internet users – an impressive number and growing. Did you know that 67% of the world's population[26] has a mobile phone, that is, c.4.5Bn people?

With mobile phone companies offering subscription computing bundles (a PC on a mobile phone contract) this brings affordable computing to new audiences (who are more interested in what I 'can do' rather then 'how it works') that will be interested in the convenience and affordability of MS Online.

Many more mobile phone users will already have a computer connected to the Internet and see their mobile phone as the portable, lives in the pocket or handbag, convenience device. They will want services that are available when they are online at their PC also delivered to their mobile phone.

It is already forecast that mobile phone connectivity to the Internet will overtake PC connectivity so this is a high growth market.

This is a huge global customer audience – no wonder there is so much interest in online services.

Mega Mega Trends

What is the future of software? It would be folly to make statements of fact, but here is a thought.

With the assumption that all enterprise software will need to be re-written in the next 15 - 20 years then you have a software industry in transformation. As you think about all new software developments what use cases would you consider?

With 4.5Bn people having a computer in the form of a mobile phone that gets more powerful with every new generation of handset, one use case is how you deliver software to this vast audience.

For a long time the industry has talked the convergence of data and voice but we are much more advanced and now describe this convergence as Unified Communications. With a mobile device

---

[26] Source United Nations: http://www.un.org/News/briefings/docs/2010/100223_ITU.doc.htm

you are online and connected and more possibilities open up to deliver an array of services – online services.

The future points to online services.

What are customers saying?

While the IT industry gathers around the Cloud it is interesting to look at what customers are saying and, importantly, what they say about BPOS.

There have been some interesting developments around the world with some key public figures putting their cards on the table.

There have been some interesting developments around the world with some key public figures putting their cards on the table.

Steve Ballmer, CEO, Microsoft

"We're all in."

I'm all about the cloud computing notion. I look at my lifestyle, and I want access to information wherever I am. I am killing projects that don't investigate software as a service first." His report 'State of Public Sector Cloud Computing'[1] is an interesting source of public sector case studies.

Vivek Kundra

Federal CIO

The White House

John Suffolk, UK Government's CIO

A fan of SaaS. He is heading up the establishment of a UK onshore, private Government Cloud Computing Infrastructure called G-Cloud. The Australian government has expressed interest in this work.

Karen Dallyn, Services Partner Manager, BT Engage

As an expert Systems Integrator, the decision to add MS Online to our portfolio was simple. We adopted the solution early and as a result have a decent number of wins under our belt. If we weren't offering MS Online as an option to our customers, we wouldn't maintain our position as a trusted advisor.

Markus Strauss, Head of Information Technology, Real Insurance

Microsoft Online Services provides us with a robust and available business tool that we couldn't afford to build ourselves. Even better, a high level of service was available from day one and as our business grows, we only pay for what we need.

Dr. Adrian Cohen, CEO, Immediate Assistants

Microsoft Online Services has delivered us high availability, comprehensive security and simplified IT management. It has revolutionized the way we communicate, the clarity of our communications, the ease of our interactions and has dramatically reduced our IT spend.

Xtralis CIO, Simarjit Chhabra

Microsoft Online Services has delivered a business collaboration and content storage system that is flexible and scalable at a fraction of the cost and time of an in-house system. We were so pleased with the system that we paid for it a year in advance.

Josef Farnik, Managing Director and Chief Executive Officer, Spotless

With Microsoft Online Services, we can build better employee relationships and forge a more cohesive corporation that mobilizes quickly to increase market share and drive our competitive advantage.

Chapter

4

Show me the money

Seize the moment of excited curiosity on any subject to solve your doubts; for if you let it pass, the desire may never return, and you may remain in ignorance.

William Wirt (US Politician, 1772 - 1834)

T HE availability of MS Online has created some tension for partners about how they incorporate this in their portfolio to earn money and grow their business.

The Cloud and online services are no longer a new idea yet at the same time the market cannot be described as mature yet. If you see an opportunity and act whilst others look on then you will want to understand how you profit and so - show me the money.

It has always been the case that Microsoft software products have been an engine to drive partner revenues and customarily that is spoken as licensed software revenue being the driver of a partner's professional services revenues – and this remains true with MS Online.

With MS Online the accounting for software revenue is different as you are paid fees as the PoR. Your big opportunity with MS Online is to develop the skills and experience to offer your customers the choices and combinations of Software-plus-Services: on-premises deployment, partner hosted and Microsoft Online Services such as BPOS. This drives the need among customers for training and a range of professional services as we go on to describe next.

More choices for your customers drive more discussions leading to more opportunity for you. Does that sound interesting?

Significant investments have been made by Microsoft to provide the core infrastructure – a quality hosted platform – for MS Online that have broad appeal and drive the requirement for a range of professional services to be delivered to customers by Microsoft partners – i.e. you.

In this chapter we look at what professional services will be in demand by MS Online customers.

We have, as a reminder, used 'professional services' to describe the services sold by a partner (you) to a MS Online customer.

The Online customer

The relationship between customers and vendors is changing where increasingly customers locate vendors. So before we look at your professional services opportunity there are some characteristics of customers for online services like MS Online that need to be recognized.

Before the Internet customers relied heavily upon vendors for information and advice about products and services that they could use in their businesses. This allowed vendors to selectively sift information and reveal it to customers in such a way that the vendor created maximum impact to close the sale.

Today the Internet has empowered your customers with search, blogs, and wikis and as a result there has been a shift in the balance of power you have as a vendor to reveal information. If your customer is looking for products, services, advice or is problem solving then the Internet will serve it up in a matter of seconds.

It is highly probable they already know about the Cloud and MS Online and are curious what it means for their business which means that your customers are better informed than ever – Caveat Venditor as opposed to Caveat Emptor![27]

> **Cloud computing**
>
> Bing returns 26M+ results when searched on "cloud computing" – perhaps too much information? How can you help?

---

[27] *http://en.wikipedia.org/wiki/Caveat_emptor*

Just as sales behavior adapts to markets so too does buyer behavior. Put yourself in the role of a potential buyer of BPOS and live the customer experience. Be Online wise.

Put money in your customers' pocket

The SMB is the backbone of many economies. In a previous chapter we referenced the Microsoft SMB survey (February 2010) and here we expand on what the survey revealed and other information that is shaping the world we operate in.

In a World Economic Forum: Global Information Technology Report 2009-10[28], it was reported in the Executive Summary that the ICT industry has become an increasingly important industry in the global economy, accounting for approximately 5 percent of total GDP growth between 2003 and 2008 and representing 5.4 percent of GDP worldwide in 2008. It goes on to report the potential impact of the Cloud on economic growth through start-up of new businesses and resulting job creation. It specifically points out that the Cloud is suited to help start-up businesses to equip with ICT at a price they can afford when cash is in short supply. This is being played out with Venture Capital firms now insisting that the businesses they invest in use the Cloud so more cash can be put into R&D and sales and marketing operations. If this formula works for start-up businesses then surely it applies to most SMB businesses – unless they have mountains of cash?

The report assesses the impact of the Cloud, where for example in Europe, it could create 1M+ jobs over the next five 5 years and that gets the attention of governments. For this upbeat forecast to materialize it will require investment to deliver a fast and reliable network to carry data, voice and images whether you are at the workplace, at home or on the road. This will foster a relationship between governments and the private sector to deliver the infrastructure that will deliver on creation of jobs.

Governments have witnessed the tremendous impact that the Internet has had and are now scouting the opportunity of the Cloud. This is no longer a 'watch this space' but a 'be part of it'.

---

[28] *http://www.weforum.org/en/initiatives/gcp/Global%20Information%20Technology%20Report/index.htm*

This report also includes a Networked Readiness Index 2009–2010 a table that ranks the capabilities of 133 countries (representing 98% of World GDP) to deliver the infrastructure for online (in the Cloud) business.

Why is this important?

IT is a vital resource and the assumption, actually requirement, is that it is always available when you need it. If network connectivity is essential to access those IT resources then it had better be guaranteed. As with any major new advancement there will be growing pains to meet the appetite of demand and the economic incentives are there for government and the private sector to respond.

At a 'my business' level do you benefit from the availability of online services?

In the Microsoft end-user survey[29] (published February 3rd 2010) among SMB customers, Microsoft looked at this with an interesting slant as they looked for evidence to correlate customers adoption of SaaS (referred to as hosted services in their survey) and their financial performance.

The headline statement for this survey was: Microsoft Study Reveals Small and Midsize Businesses Using Hosted Services Have Better Financial Performance. *Uh! That was unexpected!*

In the detail they reported more than 40 percent of the respondents that use hosted or cloud technology reported revenue rises of 30 percent or more compared with 90 percent of respondents not using hosted technology that saw decreases in revenue. *This is important news.*

Would this influence the conversation that you have with your customers?

To the other part; if your customers had this information what conversation do you think they would like to have with you?

This section was headed up: Put money in your customers' pocket.

You will need a plan to act on this information but before we go to that think about working 'on' your business not 'in' your business.

---

[29] *http://www.microsoft.com/presspass/press/2010/feb10/02-03TechCriticalPR.mspx*

This expression brings to the attention that in the commotion of the business day we get absorbed with what needs to be done 'in' the business.

Think about your 'end game'.

Meantime the world keeps spinning around and time passes and so it is good practice to set aside time, regular time, to work 'on' your business. This frees up the mind to explore: *What's coming up? What's changing that affects our customers and our business opportunities? What significant news/events have we about our customers? Do we look out for customers' news /events and how should we act on that? When did we last take a refreshing conversation to our customers and have a favorable response?*

Here are four things to do to make ready for that conversation:

1.	Know if your customer is using hosted services and, if they do, their business justification for making that decision.
2.	Find out what IT represents as a % of your customer's revenue and benchmark that against other customers with the knowledge acquired through 1 above.
3.	Profile you customer's IT usage using the suggested outline in Chapter 2 and identify applications they use and for that matter do not use that are available as hosted services and price them.
4.	Look at the applications identified in 3 and compare the current cost to bring the on-premises implementation of those applications up to the same level available from a hosted service. In the case of existing installed systems on-premises that may require hardware and software upgrades. To access the hosted service may require the installation of a supported browser (usually free to download) on existing PCs and a reassessment of network bandwidth to deliver a good user experience.

Can you now identify applications that deliver new and improved functionality delivered as a hosted service with the confidence of a SLA to your customer that improves the economics of your customer's business?

Go further: What is the potential impact for the customer's existing IT assets where some applications are moved online as a hosted service? Will this free up resources to deliver improved performance for those applications that must reside on-premises?

As the world emerges from recession do you expect your customers to return to normal pre-recession buying habits or will they have had a re-think? Perhaps it is timely to re-think your role and be creative about how you demonstrate your value to your customers.

As every business knows; with change there is opportunity and timing is everything.

More choices, more customers

Your customers know Microsoft and the solutions that you have provided are part of the DNA of their businesses. They rely upon you to provide a range of service to maintain hardware and software and fix things when they go wrong.

They are getting on with their business and like to think that you will look out for opportunities that will offer improvements and save them money.

MS Online services

Microsoft hosts MS Online so the complexity associated with the maintenance, management and operation of servers is removed. This alleviates a partner of some activities that you are accustomed to performing for your customers but you might consider this change also removes some risks and costs you assumed in the provision of some services, e.g. break – fix agreements, SLAs.

There are some changes to the professional services applicable for customers using MS Online and these are explained later in this Chapter.

On-premise

Your current deal with your customer is to supply them hardware and software and upgrade and replace it over time. Depending on the skills and resources of your customers you may provide installation services, help desk and problem resolution, hardware maintenance, software support, consulting services, training services and more and as long as your customers remain in business you see no end to this.

Your customers have IT on-premises and you are actively involved and they pay you to make it work and keep it working. This is your professional services business and many aspects remain with MS Online.

Partner Hosted

A key part of the Microsoft Software-plus-Services story is the partner hosted element. This is not the focus of this book. It may be the case that capabilities required by your customer cannot be provided through MS Online services and in that case a partner hosted service may be the answer.

Your initial reaction might be: this looks to be game changing and I need to know the full implications for my business and quickly.

 In truth the IT industry lives and breathes innovation and that has been the driver for many new businesses and the growth of established businesses. Would you agree?

The attraction of subscription pricing makes online services more accessible and affordable so your customers can increase the use of IT in their business and with that your opportunity to provide related professional services.

 MS Online subscription pricing removes one of the barriers that limit your customers' use of IT – upfront cost.

How often has your customer said: *"if we could afford it"*, *"if we could justify it"*, *"if the ROI were better"* and *"let's talk again when business picks up"*

Well now you have a new approach to these questions with MS Online. In the prevailing economic conditions you may view MS Online as a good news story?

MS Online – priced to attract customers

Microsoft set the price for MS Online and as the PoR you will earn PoR fees when your customers subscribe to MS Online.

> Your customers already meet the cost of a number of business essentials through a pay per use/consumption pricing model (gas, electricity, telephony, rent etc.).
>
> By offering MS Online with its subscription pricing you are 'pushing on an open door'.

The PoR fee income is recurring provided that you remain the PoR and your customers remain under contract and that will grow cumulatively with the acquisition of new customers over time. Bear in mind that the fees you receive as the PoR will be the smaller part of your earnings opportunity with MS Online – the bigger opportunity is delivering professional services.

 MS Online is attracting customers and partners wanting to sell MS Online – don't delay your decision and let someone else get to your customers first.

Finding customers for BPOS

You are in business to make money so let's not lose sight of the fact that you need customers. So how do you find them?

One misconception about online services is that it will present a *this* or *that* choice for customers.

 OR

On-premises   **Online**

That is not the case and a number of scenarios will exist as customers mix and match on-premises and online solutions to meet their business requirements.

Some customers, particularly among small businesses may find all of their requirements met by online services.

ALL

Online

Many customers will combine on-premises and online services.

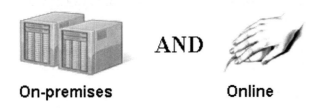

On-premises   **Online**

It is likely that migrations will occur from on-premises to online services and vice-versa as dictated by changing business requirements. Mergers, acquisitions, project-based businesses and new business ventures all fall in this category.

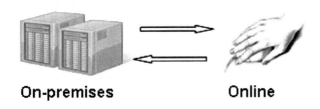

On-premises   **Online**

One thing for sure is that choice will open up new opportunities for customers and in turn for you to develop solutions and offer professional services that optimize how your customers use on-premises and online services.

In summary your opportunities will be found among customers:

- moving existing on-premises services to online services

- adding new online services that were neither affordable nor justifiable if implemented on-premises

- combining on-premises and online services to create an optimal cost/benefit solution

- adding users that were not justified under the economics of licensed software but now affordable with online services

- attracted to the convenience (IT made easy!) and affordability of online services

- your initiative to research your customers and formulate choices that change the economics of IT for their businesses

- new users known as Deskless Workers – the workers that do not sit at desks and often found in customer service roles

 We describe above MS Online licensing opportunities that signal your opportunity to offer a range of professional services to customers. Would that make a difference?

Your professional services might include: training, a managed service[30] to alleviate your customers of the day to day IT administration and support of users, integration where required with other applications, customization (e.g. of SharePoint) and migration to MS Online.

IT is a key resource and your customers are constantly looking for ways to extract value for their business and your opportunity to engage in that discussion is now enhanced with the availability of MS Online – and why wouldn't you?

Your Opportunity

The following table is a non-exhaustive summary of these opportunities. Where there is a tick in the customer and partner columns there is the possibility of either performing that activity. However in the case of a SMB customer they may want a partner

---

[30] A managed service as defined by Wikipedia is the practice of transferring day-to-day related *management* responsibility as a *strategic* method for improved effective and efficient operations.

to be involved in the administration of the service, in part due to the lower probability of the customer having the required IT skills to do so. It is not a requirement that a customer involve the PoR in the case of a support request but you will often be far better positioned to determine if that request should be submitted to Microsoft, should be dealt with through the Administration Portal or in fact is a local on-premise issue.

Your knowledge of things that your customers do not know nor have the skills or time to devote to is your opportunity to make a bid - don't wait to be asked make your customer a proposal.

Activity: BPOS specific	Customer does it	Partner does it	MS Online does it
Requirements analysis/ consulting.		✓	
Project planning		✓	
Sign up for a 30 day trial of BPOS. Purchase of BPOS and purchase of additional users	✓		
Migration of users accounts from an existing Active Directory domain to BPOS		✓	
Creation and deletion of BPOS mailbox enabled user accounts		✓	
Resetting of user passwords	✓	✓	
Installing and managing client software – both BPOS specific such as the sign in tool and other general desktop software		✓	
Internet DNS management such as the modification of MX records and domain names		✓	

Activity: BPOS specific	Customer does it	Partner does it	MS Online does it
Migration of email accounts from an existing mail server/service to BPOS		✓	
Exchange service maintenance including performance monitoring, patching and data centre level backups			✓
Management of email anti-virus			✓
Management of the customers anti-spam block and allow lists		✓	
Configuration of optional Exchange Hosted Archiving		✓	
Implementing email distribution lists, contacts and meeting rooms.		✓	
Recovery of accidently deleted mail items (up to 14 days)	✓		
Recovery of an accidently deleted user account and mailbox (up to 30 days)			✓
Recovery of a corrupted mail item or mailbox (up to 14 days)			✓
Increasing the mailbox size of a BPOS user		✓	
Creating SharePoint site collections		✓	
SharePoint site collection administration including security, initial features, content types and navigation		✓	

Activity: BPOS specific	Customer does it	Partner does it	MS Online does it
SharePoint Customization using browser based tools and SharePoint Designer		✓	
Creation of the top level sites within a site collection		✓	
Creation and management of lower level sub sites within SharePoint	✓	✓	
Addition and management of SharePoint site content such as documents and meetings	✓		
Recovery of a recently deleted SharePoint file, list or item (up to 30 days)	✓		
Recovery of accidently deleted SharePoint site from client side backup		✓	
Management of longer term SharePoint site archiving and backup using client tools (over 30 days)		✓	
Management of SharePoint antivirus			✓
SharePoint service maintenance including performance monitoring, patching and data centre level backups			✓
Setting up Live Meeting rooms	✓		
Management of on-premise Active Directory		✓	

Activity: BPOS specific	Customer does it	Partner does it	MS Online does it
Management of on-premise network components and internet connection		✓	
Management of in house applications and databases		✓	
Management of customers' public website		✓	
Product and Business Process Training		✓	

Managed Service Opportunity

As the table reveals there is commonality between the professional services that you already provide to customers on-premises with those that are needed by customers using MS Online services. This means that all your existing skills are transferrable to customers that use MS Online services.

Managed services are chargeable services and a source of recurring revenue and as a PoR you have the opportunity to earn from the services you provide as 1st line support and other services (e.g. help desk) to your customers.

The idea of generating a significant proportion of your revenues from services may be new to you but understand the global economy is dependant upon services industries that make up an estimated 67% of world GDP. In 2009 the services industries of the USA comprised an estimated 76.9% of GDP[31].

 Equate services you provide with an economic value to your customers and set an appropriate price. If the world didn't do this the global economy would be busted.

For those activities that Microsoft performs you would typically, where you offer a managed service, be the first point of contact for

---

[31] Source Central Intelligence Agency at www.cia.gov

your customer and you would escalate the request to Microsoft as appropriate.

For example, if your customer reported to you that certain email items were corrupted you would collect as much information about the lost items as possible and then initiate a service request from within the BPOS administration portal.

This is only the beginning as online services expand over time with new functionality and additional products your managed services opportunity expands. Your investment in BPOS is the foundation for growing your business with MS Online.

 Consider the impact of the recurring revenue opportunities from managed services combined with PoR fees earned to grow your business.

It is important to note that some partners may not be in the position to provide a managed service offering to a customer and in that case the customer can request support directly from Microsoft. This means that you can sell BPOS even if you do not have today or intend to have the way to provide a managed service to customers.

BPOS partner revenues

Knowledge is accumulating from partners that have made sales of BPOS to understand the composition of the revenue streams that BPOS sales had generated.

Interestingly, sales of BPOS to enterprise customers featured strongly in the evidence. That said it is likely the case that enterprise customers will drive greater opportunities for professional services revenues and therefore these examples should be thought of as indicative.

The table below categorizes known BPOS revenue streams.

Partner of Record (PoR) fees	*Annuity*
Migration and Integration	*Usually one-time*
Customization and Consultancy	*On-going*
Managed Services	*Recurrent*

Analysis of 40 US BPOS deals won over a 6 month timeline with a 141 user average deal size generated a distribution of revenue per the chart below.

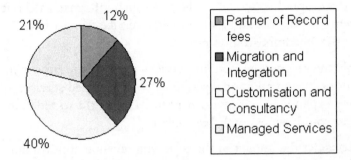

The percentages in the table above highlight that PoR fees are the smaller part of total revenues but remember the PoR fees are recurrent.

Some partners have concerns that PoR fees are insubstantial and this is acting as a deterrent to selling BPOS. This is not the case as the table above shows. The revenue analysis behind the above table shows every $1 earned in PoR fees driving $7 in professional services revenue. While this is a snapshot it evidences that PoR fees are one part of the revenue available to a partner but of course you have to sell BPOS to trigger the PoR fees and associated professional services revenue opportunity.

A senior executive of a partner that is selling BPOS puts an interesting spin on how the PoR fees they earn is transforming their gross margin and provides a foundation for budget planning in the year ahead. They remarked that...

PoR fees are earned at negligible cost and offer 100% gross margin. As PoR fees are recurring they are a predictable revenue stream on which to base costs and that is very useful to financial planning.

This is one point of view from a partner that is selling BPOS and who speaks from experience. There are many case studies for both customers and partners and that is referenced in chapter 10.

Migration to BPOS

Most existing Microsoft partners who sell BPOS inform their biggest money earner so far has been the resulting migration projects.

The migration to BPOS can be split into a number of steps to include: planning, network assessment, account synchronization, mail migration and data migration. A plan for off-boarding would also be expected in case of a later change of direction (e.g. a move back to on-premises) at a future date. Questions about migration are covered in chapter 7.3.

Building an Intranet with SharePoint Online

Getting involved in building a customer's SharePoint Online intranet portal is a great way to earn additional revenue and build on your strength as the PoR.

Many organizations have implemented SharePoint over the last few years for a number of good reasons – it solves the workaday requirements of document creation, collaboration, search and retrieval. As a result it has become Microsoft's fastest product to reach $1Bn in sales.

Customers like SharePoint for its document management capabilities, varied collaboration features, search, as an intranet replacement and, for some, to build custom business applications. As things change over time, perhaps driven by user experiences or changing business needs, it leads to requests for feature enhancements and refinements to business processes as SharePoint supports the workforce to conduct their day to day business. All through this life cycle it brings in scope requirements to consult, plan, build, educate, support and document SharePoint – all work that you as a partner can earn money from providing.

Questions about building an Intranet with SharePoint Online are covered in section 7.4.

Your choice – Your money

Do you:

 Pretend it is not happening and that your customers will have no interest in the Cloud and MS Online?

OR

 Accept reality that the Cloud is going to shape the future of how your customers use software and embrace MS Online?

If you don't act for your customers then it is highly likely that someone else will.

This book was written to help you decide.

Ask the Smart Questions

If I have seen further it is by standing on the shoulders of giants

Isaac Newton (Scientist, 1643 – 1727)

SMART Questions is about giving you valuable insights or "the Smarts". Normally these are only gained through years of painful and costly experience. Whether you already have a general understanding of the subject and need to take it to the next level or are starting from scratch, you need to make sure you ask the Smart Questions. And the ideal time to "Ask the Smart Questions" is while you are still "Thinking of...." and not as a response to problems after you have jumped. We aim to short circuit that learning process, by providing the expertise of the 'giants' that Isaac Newton referred to.

Not all the questions will necessarily be new or staggeringly insightful. The value you get from the information will clearly vary. It depends on your job role and previous experience. We call this the 3Rs.

The 3 Rs

1. Some of the questions will be in areas where you know all the answers so they will be **Reinforced** in your mind.

2. You may have forgotten certain areas so the book will **Remind** you.

3. And other questions may be things you've never considered and will be **Revealed** to you.

How do you use Smart Questions?

The structure of the questions is set out in Chapter 6, and the questions are laid out in tables in Chapters 7 and 8. In the table you have the basic question and then the reason why you should care. We've also provided a helpful checkbox so that you can mark which questions are relevant to your particular situation.

A quick scan down the list of questions should give you a general feel of where you are for each question vs. the 3Rs[32].

At the highest level they are a sanity check or checklist of areas to consider. You can take them with you to meetings or copy to others in the business for comment or advice. Each question is uniquely numbered to collate replies. It might be one question alone saves you a whole heap of cash or heartache – as in "did you remember to turn the gas off?"

In Chapters 9, 10 and 11 we've tried to bring some of the questions to life with anecdotes and stories.

There may be some 'aha' moments. Hopefully not too many sickening, 'head in the hands – what have we done' moments, where you've realized that your company is hopelessly exposed. If you're in that situation, then the questions will help you negotiate yourself back into control.

In this context, probably the most critical role of the questions is to present a balanced perspective to guide you in your deliberation about what really matters and why that is.

Hopefully they should open up your thinking to opportunities that you hadn't necessarily considered. Balancing the opportunities and the risks, and then agreeing what is realistically achievable is the key to formulating strategy.

Every decision in life is shaped by our emotions, experience and instincts and we don't attempt to change this rather just give you the benefit of being able to see round some corners.

---

[32] Or whether you need the For Dummies book (which we haven't written)

How to dig deeper

Need more information? Not convinced by the examples, or want ones that are more relevant to you specific situation? The Smart Questions micro-site for the book has a list of other supporting material. As this subject is moving quickly many of the links are to websites or blogs.

And of course there is a community of people who've read the book and are all at different levels of maturity who have been brought together on the Smart Questions micro-site for the book.

And finally

Please remember that these questions are NOT intended to be a prescriptive list that must be followed slavishly from beginning to end. It is inevitable that the list of questions is not exhaustive and we are confident that with the help of the community the list of Smart Questions will grow.

If you want to rephrase a question to improve its context or have identified a question we've missed, then let us know and add to the collective knowledge.

We also understand that not all of the questions will apply to all businesses. However we encourage you to read them all as there may be a nugget of truth that can be adapted to your circumstances.

Above all we hope that this book provides a guide or a pointer to the areas that may be valuable to you and helps with the "3 Rs".

Chapter

6

This probably can't wait - Questions

One's first step in wisdom is to question everything - and one's last is to come to terms with everything.

Georg Christoph Lichtenberg (1742 – 1799)

OUR purpose is to put you in the driving seat and provide you the information to assess if MS Online is something that can wait or needs your attention now.

To help you we have provided you questions that will guide you to make the right decision.

Chapter 7: Questions about MS Online

1. Questions for my business

2. Questions about my customers

3. Questions about migrating to BPOS

4. Questions about SharePoint Online

Chapter 8: Questions about selling MS Online

1. Questions for sales organizations

2. Questions for service organizations

Chapter

7

Questions about MS Online

It is better to know some of the questions than all of the answers.

James Thurber (US author, cartoonist, humorist, & satirist 1894 - 1961)

YOU want to do the right thing by your customers but also the right thing for your business. You may see MS Online in the light of opportunity or a big unknown? Whatever you initial thoughts in this chapter we help you work through deciding what is important for your business.

The availability of MS Online marks change for Microsoft partners and while that may be uncomfortable that is only true until a decision has been made about MS Online – to make it part of your portfolio of products and services - or not?

This is the backdrop for the following questions that are designed to help you work through the opportunity, change and impact for your business.

It is imperative you have a position about online services in preparation for conversations that you will have with investors, employees, commentators and your customers.

Previously that has been hard as the delivery of online services has many moving parts (it is complex) and requires large upfront capital investment. Now Microsoft's has made it easy for partners to sell online services and start earning with MS Online for a small investment of time in training and an immediate start.

7.1 Questions for my business

You want to do the right thing by your customers but also the right thing for your business.

Along comes MS Online and you need a sense of what this means to your business?

You need help to quickly make an informed decision – why wait?

keep it simple …. help me work it out for myself …. if you use jargon keep it to a minimum and explain it so I can tell others …. maybe just one or two **TLA** to remember and no more …. put things into perspective for me …. and for my customers when I meet them …. help me with what I don't know but need to know …. I'm smart not stupid …. let's get on with it

☒	Question	Why this matters
☐	7.1.1 Is the market ready for MS Online?	Judging the time to enter a market opportunity is a critical part of business planning and execution. Do you see value in first mover advantage? Do you prefer to join a market when it moves with a herd instinct? Or are you of the opinion that: If customers are buying then the market is ready.
☐	7.1.2 Is this the right time to enter the market with MS Online?	Timing in business is often a mix of skill and luck. Don't be lulled into inaction; I'm not ready so my customers can't be ready either. In this book there are many examples of how to look for information to assess the opportunities and that will help you decide the timing question. What do you read in the business pages about IT trends? Have you performed some random searches using BING on "BPOS", "SaaS", and "cloud computing" so you read what you customers might read?
☐	7.1.3 What else do I need to consider?	In cold reality the question is: do you believe that in the next 12 - 24 months that online services will be something that just faded away (a passing fad) or a major influence on how customers specify and buy IT? It is one of those moments when you get to call it right or wrong. We provide the clues - you decide.

☒	Question	Why this matters
☐	7.1.4 How do I start to evaluate BPOS opportunities with my existing customers?	BPOS offers an alternative to on-premises installation of hardware and software. So, for example, it may be the case that your customer does not use SharePoint because of the limitations of the associated costs when installed on-premises. A quick way to evaluate where opportunities exist with current customers is to perform an audit of the products they have installed and compare this with the list of products available with BPOS – a 'map and gap' analysis.
☐	7.1.5 Will BPOS change the services that I offer?	If you already sell and support the products that comprise BPOS then you are in a great position to support BPOS customers. The specific services you offer a BPOS customer will be like those you offer any customer that you currently provide 1st line support. The big difference is that there is no server to support as the applications are hosted by Microsoft. One consequence of this is to likely reduce the need to go on-site. More of your time with a customer will involve supporting users by telephone or engaging in a Live Meeting.
☐	7.1.6 Will BPOS be of interest to my existing customers?	Yes very likely and they will attract the interest of others that sell BPOS. It is often said it is easier and the cost of sale is dramatically reduced when selling to an existing customer. So you may want to defend your position in existing customers from others offering BPOS and competitors with rival hosted services. Analysis of BPOS sales confirm that customers with Microsoft licensed software products installed on-premises are buying BPOS and that includes SMB and Enterprise customers.

☒	**Question**	**Why this matters**
☐	7.1.7 Will BPOS impact my revenues?	The IT industry has been through 6[33] major technological disruptions and each time that changed the opportunity to earn money. You let go some of the past to renew. How did you answer 7.1.3? If 20% of your customers buy MS Online in the next 12 months and you were <u>not</u> the provider (PoR) for those services what impact would that have on your revenues?
☐	7.1.8 Where are my current customers based?	MS Online customers can choose their PoR from any country where MS Online is currently available (in 39 countries). If you have customers with multiple country locations you will need to decide if you wish to increase your geographic focus and in particular how that impacts how you to deliver customer service/support.
☐	7.1.9 What is the opportunity with Software-plus-Services?	Software-plus-Services present new ways to combine existing investments made by your customers with opportunities MS Online and the Cloud. So it provides protection of investment with scope for you to bring new ideas to your customer. See 7.2.

---

[33] Depending on your age and longevity in the industry and your point of view you will recall:
1. Mainframe 2. Minicomputer 3. Personal Computer (a turning point for the IT industry)
4. Networked Personal Computer 5. Mobile Phone (a computer!) 6. Internet/SaaS/Cloud (profound implications still unfolding).

☒	Question	Why this matters
☐	7.1.10 Capex or Opex does it matter?	Capex is capital expenditure that creates a future benefit and are costs that cannot be deducted in the year in which they are paid or incurred, and must be capitalized. Opex is operating expenditure and classed as ongoing expenses in the business. The payment of BPOS subscriptions by your customers is treated as Opex. You need to understand the investment climate and business justification 'hurdles' that dictates your customers' spending on IT to know whether Capex or Opex is the driver for decision making. You in turn need to understand the resulting accounting implications for your business on your P&L and cash flow.
☐	7.1.11 How do I profit from Software-plus-Services?	When your customers combine on-premises with MS Online it breaks through one of the barriers that limits your customers' use of IT – the cost to their business. Subscription based pricing makes MS Online more accessible and affordable so your customers can increase the use of IT in their business. As they increase the use of IT your opportunity grows to provide professional services. Studies also show that as customers shift IT spend from Capex to Opex then they are more inclined to spend on managed services with partners.

☒	Question	Why this matters
☐	7.1.12 Is MS Online something I should use in my business?	While we are looking at upside it bears consideration to look at this as an option. Are you due an upgrade to Microsoft 2010 Versions? Are there MS Online products that you do not use today but would consider using if provided as a MS Online service? If you used MS Online in your business do you consider it would enhance your capability to sell to and support MS Online customers?
☐	7.1.13 What services will be in demand by MS Online customers?	Aligning the right MS Online services to the needs of customers is important as is an understanding of the professional services that will be required to combine MS Online with a customer's existing IT investments. You are now aligning your business with the delivery of Software-plus-Services and that presents opportunities for: customization, integration, migration and managed services. This is expanded upon in 7.2.
☐	7.1.14 How does MS Online affect the sale of software licenses?	As you look to create scenarios with customers and their future purchases of licensed software and MS Online, that will have an effect on revenue and margin. Microsoft had developed a tool to assist partners to calculate profits from MS Online, see Appendix at the back of the book.

☒	Question	Why this matters
☐	7.1.15 What are the likely implications if I put off my decision to sell MS Online for say 12 months?	An audit of your existing customers and the applications that they have compared with those available with MS Online will highlight areas of opportunity and threat. The opportunity arises from talking to customers about how new applications can be acquired with MS Online. The threat arises from others talking to your customers about the same applications and you are not engaged in that conversation. Also think about how MS Online would help you to win new business.
☐	7.1.16 What are the major impacts of MS Online on my business?	MS Online changes the mix of license to service revenue that you are accustomed to. It will skew towards services because as the PoR you will be paid PoR fees by Microsoft rather than earn the revenue from the sale of Microsoft licensed software products. In turn this will cause adjustments to the cash flow that you have customarily earned from the sale of licensed software. This is potentially game changing.
☐	7.1.17 Who does the customer contract with for MS Online?	Microsoft. The customer pays Microsoft and they pay to you fees as the PoR. All other services and professional services provided by you to MS Online customers will be on your own terms of business.

☒	Question	Why this matters
☐	7.1.18 How will Microsoft drive business to me?	Customer cost of acquisition impacts cost of sales and your P&L. The margin you earn from the sale of MS Online is fixed. Your upside is the professional services that you provide customers where you determine the price. When a customer signs up for a trial or purchase of MS Online they are prompted to enter a PoR. Ensuring that your partner profile and Pinpoint[34] entries are up to-date is essential to win customers. Bear in mind that your existing customers also present MS Online opportunities and for them to name you as their PoR. Read again the information in this book about the Partner Sales Portal.
☐	7.1.19 What alternatives are there to MS Online?	That depends whether you are already a hosting provider? If you are then you will be in a position to compare your offer with MS Online and how you target each to your customers. If you are not a hosting provider then MS Online presents you the opportunity today to offer hosted services backed by Microsoft. You have the flexibility to offer the solution that is right for your customer. And don't forget if you don't talk to your customers about the options then others offering competitive solutions just may!
	7.1.20 What do I do if I want to start selling MS Online?	1. You need to be a member of the Microsoft Partner Network (MPN) 2. Accept the Microsoft Online Service Partner Agreement (MOSPA) on the MPN 3. Complete online training and assessment 4. Start selling and earning money

[34] Pinpoint is a major initiative to streamline the number of places that a partner can promote their services to customers and other partners. This is being rolled out globally and more information can be found at *http://pinpoint.microsoft.com*

☒ **Question**	**Why this matters**
☐ 7.1.21 What if I have no time to consider this now?	If you can't say Yes or No at this time then at least formulate a position and clarify that on your web site and with all employees so that you have a consistent message to customers. Don't allow your customers to think you have no interest. At least put a remark on your web site so customers can contact you about MS Online if they need to.
☐ 7.1.22 Is there anything else?	Look to your customers. We developed - Questions about my customers - for this reason.

Top 5 benefits for MS Online partners

1. Recurring monthly revenue. Delivers predictability for the balance sheet.

2. Remote customer support. Support teams are relieved of travelling time to customer so are more productive.

3. All customers on same software release. This simplifies the delivery of support and increases service revenue opportunities as all customers migrate simultaneously with new releases of MS Online.

4. New selling opportunities. MS Online is priced to attract customers and trials can be proposed to start-up a sales campaign. The initial (12 month) term commitment by a customer to MS Online keeps customers' costs low and allow them to proceed with a project that might not pass the test for capital expenditure.

5. Services. MS Online is the driver for a range of professional services and consultancy delivered by you to your customers.

Many of the questions before and in 7.2 will help you decide how applicable and accessible these benefits are to your business.

7.2 Questions about my customers

It took 75 years for telephones to be used by 50 million customers, but it took only four years for the Internet to reach that many users.

Those in hi-tech businesses know all about change and how rapidly change can make or break a business.

Perhaps your customers are already using online services – *you would know that?*

We all love customers but trying to second guess them is one dangerous game.

In sales we come to accept irony in spite of all our training and instincts to qualify our customers' needs, wants and desires. Things sometimes happen and often times that is, if we were truthful, because we chose not to accept some possibilities since their outcomes did not suit our end game. For example, you don't feel ready to offer online services but even though your customer is convinced you steer them away from online services. Your customer buys online services anyway. Now you are in a hard place.

This section is about putting your feet in the shoes of your customers and opening up to possibilities that might sway your customers and contemplating their irony: we know why we invest in IT and if we have a choice to own and operate (on-premises) or pay a subscription for online services - which would be better for our business and why?

Customers are ready for this conversation – and you can be ready with MS Online.

☒	Question	Why this matters
☐	7.2.1 How do I open a conversation with my customers about MS Online?	Your assumption might be; my customers know nothing about hosted services and seem content to buy hardware and software so why change? Has your customer delayed making buying decisions? Have they been reluctant to start up new discussions about forward planning for IT? Are they spending more or less with you comparing year on year? Are you looking for an opportunity to re-engage with a customer? See 7.2.3 and 7.2.4.
☐	7.2.2 Is there a right time to start a conversation about MS Online?	If you supplied hardware and software to your customer are these purchases fully depreciated? Has your customer indicated there are financial constraints on buying new, replacement and/or upgrades? The answer might be found in 7.2.3, 7.2.4. and 7.2.5.
☐	7.2.3 Has my customer asked about hosted services?	No, then don't delay in starting up a conversation even if the basis for that is sharing examples of how you are using MS Online in your business. Yes, get in there because your customer is looking for advice and experience and may even be ready to buy.
☐	7.2.4 Do I know if my customers use hosted services today?	Why should that matter? It means they have already made a decision in principle that hosted services have a role in the business. If they buy one service they are likely to buy more. It will help you to know what their reasons were to move to hosted services and what benefits they attribute to that decision. Perhaps they intend to move all their business applications to the Cloud?
☐	7.2.5 Have my customers tightened their financial review of IT spending?	The IT team love it and now the finance team get to look over the money. Problem. All Capex is held up. Perhaps in 6 months? All that work for nothing. Did you consider all the alternatives?

☒ Question	Why this matters
☐ 7.2.6 How do I qualify my customers' interest in MS Online?	Know the answer to question 7.2.4 it is indicative of their predisposition to online services. Remember MS Online is a 12 month initial commitment that allows customers to try things that might not pass a ROI test for Capex. Use MS Online in your own business this will help with inspiration to drive conversations with customers. The risk is you don't qualify their interest then someone else might.
☐ 7.2.7 Is there a situation where I should not propose MS Online to my customer?	MS Online was not designed with a specific customer segment or industry sector in mind. It delivers services in the Cloud for small and large enterprise customers alike.
☐ 7.2.8 Why would my customer pay for MS Online rather than use a free solution?	MS Online is priced aggressively but it isn't free and that means you can earn money selling MS Online. Many businesses use free internet software, such as Hotmail, Live Messenger or Google Docs. Compare what free provides your customer and what MS Online provides and expand your customers understanding of the limitations of free. For example promote: the benefit of a SLA, the assurance of a solution backed by Microsoft, your expertise, the benefit of Microsoft's industry leading R&D, the on-going availability of Microsoft's latest products, reliable support (when you need it!) for those products, enterprise security, shared calendaring , mobile access, an integrated suite, regionally targeted hosting etc. Look at the information at *http://www.whymicrosoft.com*

☒ Question	Why this matters
☐ 7.2.9 Can I arrange a trial of MS Online for my customers?	Yes a trial often leads to a sale. Get to understand their motivation for a trial. Is it simply curiosity? Is there a pressing business requirement? Be involved. It is important you guide prospective customers through the sign up process and ensure that you are named as their PoR. Be aware that your customers can start a trial without involving a PoR – try to avoid that happening.
☐ 7.2.10 Should I discourage my customers' trial of MS Online?	Maybe. Although it is common practice to offer 'try before you buy' for hosted services (that is part of their appeal), it is important that you manage your customer's experience during the trial. Your involvement during a trial can help your customer make a decision – they are on a path to make a purchase! The alternative is to leave your customer to 'experiment' and that can delay or even loose the sale. See 7.1.4 and 8.1.12 also.
☐ 7.2.11 What else do I need to be aware of?	You can influence your customers' interest and loyalty by the advice you offer about online services. To do that you will need to be aware of a number of related offerings and that information can be found in Chapters 2 and 3.
☐ 7.2.12 Can my customer change their PoR?	Yes. An MS Online customer is at liberty to change their PoR. It is therefore important that you establish a clear reason for the customer to keep you as their PoR. This is your professional services opportunity.

☒	Question	Why this matters
☐	7.2.13 Have you had discussions with your customers about high availability?	Providing highly available services is usually very expensive and the fact that MS Online offers 99.9% availability under a SLA may be a compelling reason for some customers to consider it. If any of your customers have had a recent loss of service or data this may be the time to talk about the benefits of high availability with the backing of Microsoft's SLA.
☐	7.2.14 Do you know if your customer has specific data security requirements?	MS Online provides a highly secure environment for storage of company data and email but some customers might need the details of such things as the firewall configuration or datacenter location. Others might use token or card based authentication to their services and might find the password logon that MS Online uses inappropriate for their needs.
☐	7.2.15 Do you know if your customer has specific data retention requirements?	Customers often have specific requirements related to their compliance policies and this is particularly true in regulated industries (e.g. financial services) and the public sector. For retention of email (internal and external) and IM, Microsoft Exchange Hosted Archiving is available priced on a per user per month basis. It provides an organization unlimited archive storage capacity per user for a 10-year retention term. Historical data may be included in the archive for a one-time charge.

☒	Question	Why this matters
☐	7.2.16 Does your customer ask: Where is my data stored?	It is stored in a Microsoft datacenter. Cross border data transfers of many types of data (personal and business) are commonplace. If your customer has specific requirements about 'where' (the geographical location) their data is stored then that needs to be exposed early in the sales cycle. The actual street address location of Microsoft datacenters is not revealed for security reasons. The geo-redundant datacenters are in: Amsterdam, Chicago, Dublin, Hong Kong, Japan, Quincy, San Antonio and Singapore. For a list of countries where MS Online is available and their associated data centers refer to Microsoft's Licensing and Business Policy Guide – see Appendix. If they insist the data is domicile for legal, regulatory or other contractual reason then this must be established early in the sales cycle.
☐	7.2.17 During this economic downturn what has been the thrust of my customers' conversations about IT?	Have projects that you were discussing and bidding for been dropped? Have new IT initiatives dried up? Have your customers' been laying off IT staff? What do your customers' tell you are their 'now' priorities? If cost control and cost reduction is a 'now' priority then explore where they see opportunity to make savings. Customers are very receptive to ideas that deliver cost reduction in the business and the subscription 'pay as you go' pricing of MS Online does not impact cash balances in the way that capital spending does. IT spending has not stopped it is just being directed more carefully by customers to deliver a fast return.

Top 5 benefits for customers

1. Cash flow. Monthly fees are predictable and set against operating expenditure budgets rather than capital expenditure to deliver a healthier balance sheet.

2. Availability. Financially backed Service Level Agreements provide assurances for the availability of the service.

3. Access. From anywhere there is an internet connection or mobile phone signal (or Wi-Fi if supported by the phone).

4. Convenience. You get on with your business while Microsoft takes care of the 'IT'.

5. Advantage. Affordable access to software that boosts productivity in your business.

7.3 Questions about migrating to MS Online

Perhaps your customer made the decision of their own accord or it was your initiative that led to your customer's decision to migrate to MS Online.

Partners that are selling MS Online report excellent opportunities to deliver projects with valuable consulting assignments and professional services engagement to assist customers, particularly with the migration of email to BPOS.

In this section we look at this in more detail. Every project will have its own set of unique challenges but the migration of email to BPOS has revealed many common aspects that we reveal next.

☒	Question	Why this matters
☐	7.3.1 What is the scope of the migration?	Is the whole business migrating to BPOS or just a single department or use case such as mobile workers? Is a pilot appropriate to test the migration strategy and user experience? Is this a greenfield deployment with little to no existing content to be migrated? Knowing this detail is vital to scope the Statement of Work, timescales and pricing the migration project.
☐	7.3.2 What systems does my customer have?	It is important to know your customer's migration purpose to envision their final destination. Are they reliant today using on- premise software or in a mixed environment using online services? Knowing the detail; online service providers, installed software versions and hardware levels will all help in making the migration a success and hinting at the tools you will need to use.
☐	7.3.3 What are your customer's timescales?	Your customer will usually have an expectation of when they need various stages of a migration completed by and any project needs to be planned to fit these timescales. Compromises around what is in scope and/or features may need to be made.
☐	7.3.4 What mail system is currently in place?	Mail migration is usually the most complex part of a move to BPOS and knowing and understanding a customer's existing setup is essential. A migration from an on- premise Exchange server uses different methods and tools compared to a migration from Lotus Notes or Google Mail for example. You may want to research 3rd party tools to assist with non- Exchange migrations (the number and quality of these are growing rapidly).

☒	Question	Why this matters
☐	7.3.5 Are there any other communication products currently in use?	Your customer may already use online meeting software or instant messaging. This could be provided by Microsoft in the form of Office Communication Server or Live Meeting but it's possible that is provided by another vendor such as Lotus Same Time or WebEx. Although a migration of data is probably not feasible or even required in this scenario, new client software will typically be required and user training should be planned for.
☐	7.3.6 Does the customer plan a migration or a plan for co-existence?	Co-existence scenarios where some users are moved to BPOS whilst others remain on the existing system are generally more complex to plan for and manage. Sometimes this will be for a short duration during an ongoing migration whilst at other times there will be a long term or even permanent co-existence requirement. Know this upfront so you can advise the customer accordingly.
☐	7.3.7 Have I set realistic customer expectations for migration and co-existence?	A BPOS solution will, due to its shared infrastructure, invariably have different features to an on-premise solution. This would generally be the case with any form of upgrade or solution change and BPOS is no different in this regard. Additionally co-existence has its own nuances when it comes down to how expected features work. It is important that your customer has a good understanding of the features/functions/user experience of the end solution when migrated and compared to that available during the migration and, if applicable, co-existence.

☒	Question	Why this matters
☐	7.3.8 What are the bandwidth requirements?	BPOS is a Cloud based service accessed via the Internet. Where the customer is migrating from an on-premises service to BPOS it is important to review the internet bandwidth requirements to ensure a good user experience. This may be dependent on which BPOS elements your customer is likely to use most often.
☐	7.3.9 What firewall configuration will be needed?	There is usually a limited amount of firewall configuration needed since most access to BPOS is via secure HTTPS protocol but access requirements for all BPOS users will need to be reviewed. Certain mobile devices and mail clients may need specific configuration.
☐	7.3.10 What type of directory service is in place?	The main migration tools work under the assumption that your customer has an existing on- premise Windows Active Directory deployed. If this is not the case then customized tools and methods such as CSV file import may be used. In any case having a complete picture of your customer's existing directory service is essential.
☐	7.3.11 What level of directory synchronization will be needed?	It is expected that many organizations will keep their on-premise directory services for the purpose of managing computers, security, users and other non-BPOS systems. You will need to plan for the possible ongoing synchronization of these services into BPOS and make decisions where any edits should be made to ensure consistency.

☒	Question	Why this matters
☐	7.3.12 What tools are available for user migration and synchronization?	You will need to evaluate the strengths and weaknesses of various migration tools. BPOS provides both graphical and command line (PowerShell) tools to assist with a variety of migration scenarios. You may also want to investigate 3rd party tools particularly for hosted mail to BPOS migrations.
☐	7.3.13 Does the current directory service need cleaning up first?	In order to keep the migration as simple and quick as possible it is a great idea to analyze and clean up any existing directory service in preparation for the migration.
☐	7.3.14 Which tools should I use for mail migration?	You should evaluate the various different tools and mechanisms available for migrating mailboxes and mail content. A good tool set is provided free by Microsoft but you may find additional 3rd party tools useful in some scenarios involving non-Exchange systems.
☐	7.3.15 How much mail content needs to be migrated?	You will need to discuss with your customer how much of their existing email content to migrate as 'active' and as 'archive' email. This may already be implemented within a data management policy. Is a 'big bang' or 'phased' approach preferred? Cleaning up existing mailboxes, whether done by a user or automated with techniques such as de-duplication, is recommended prior to a migration. You need to agree a plan: agreeing user migration (e.g. by department, geography, 'big bang') to BPOS, email content to be immediately available to the user after migration, whether to move other user functions such as calendars and tasks.

☒	Question	Why this matters
☐	7.3.16 Is my customer going to lose any email functionality during or after the migration?	This is something you will need to assess as early as possible. Moving a customer to BPOS only to then discover that their archiving solution no longer works as expected or that policy is not functioning is not a desirable situation. Even in an Exchange on-premise to Exchange Online migration there may be differences in functionality. It will be a case of weighing up the importance of any lost features versus the benefits of BPOS as a whole. In some cases those original features may not be required after the migration. For example, if an organization was using an archiving solution to reduce the amount of required disk space on their server then that maybe obsolete as BPOS provides 25GB of mailbox space per user.
☐	7.3.17 What options are there for migrating from other online services?	There are tools provided for migration from hosted Exchange or any POP or IMAP capable service. You may also want to look into additional 3rd party tools and services which can simplify a migration.
☐	7.3.18 What process will I use to decommission the current mail system?	The migration tools are designed to leave a copy of all content and configuration in the original destination therefore allowing you to reverse the process if needed. After a successful migration you will need to consider a cleanup process to remove older copies of mail, mailboxes and possibly mail servers. The migration tools can be used to assist with this but it will need to be planned and timed appropriately.

☒	Question	Why this matters
☐	7.3.19 What if my customer asks if it is possible to migrate out of BPOS at a later date?	There are command line tools available to help migrate content out of BPOS should the need arise and back into an on-premise system. Although hopefully not needed you should consider planning for this eventuality before the migration and particularly if it helps alleviate any of your customer's 'what if' concerns.

Microsoft has published a provisioning guide that will be updated to educate partners on the deployment and migration of services. The purpose is to assist partners to maximize the value from delivering paid for migration services. See Appendix – Online Resources for URL.

7.4 Questions about SharePoint Online

It is not as though organizations are starved of data and information rather it is the case that they struggle to organize it in a way that it can be easily found when it is needed. It is hard to remember what you called that document one year ago that you are now desperately searching for – and you really did intend to leave on time today.

Powerful indexing and search capabilities come to the rescue in the shape of SharePoint.

If your customers expose these issues then you have an open door to discuss how SharePoint can organize their data and information and get them home on time when it really matters.

With SharePoint Online this is made easy as there is no disturbance to your customer's existing IT infrastructure and comes with an opportunity to generate revenue from consulting, migration and customization of SharePoint.

In this section we look at this in more detail.

☒ Question	Why this matters
☐ 7.4.1 Has your customer implemented SharePoint?	SharePoint has been available on-premise for a number of years in both free and licensed editions. It is also part of the default installation of Small Business Server. Knowing if your customer has any experience in using SharePoint is the first step in considering moving to SharePoint Online.
☐ 7.4.2 Where does my customer keep their working documents?	One of the main reasons organizations use SharePoint is for its document management capabilities. You will need to discover where your customer currently stores their documents and how they organize collaboration on shared work. Things to consider include: • The current location of documents, e.g. file servers, local storage and within mailboxes or Exchange public folders • Existing folder structures • How are documents shared externally?
☐ 7.4.3 How much space will be needed for document storage?	SharePoint Online currently provides 250 MB per user in total space. Additional space may be purchased. You can take steps to reduce the space requirements before migration. Consider: • What is the current total space in use? • What are the average document size and how much duplication is there? • A review of current documents for labeling as 'for deletion' or 'for archive'. • Are there documents that do not need to be migrated? When moving a customer to SharePoint Online you want them to see the benefits in doing so and moving all documents wholesale rarely creates an ideal solution.

☒	Question	Why this matters
☐	7.4.4 Do they have a document archiving solution in place?	You will want to know how any archiving system works and the reasons that your customer has one before designing archiving options for SharePoint Online. In some cases you may build a new archiving solution by using SharePoint workflow or determine that archiving may be no longer required.
☐	7.4.5 What choices are there for migration of documents to SharePoint Online?	Once you have a design for the storage of documents you will need to choose a mechanism for uploading or copying files into SharePoint Online. Some organization will be best served by keeping existing documents in their current location and using SharePoint Online for the creation of new work. Others will be looking to move some or all of their existing documents to SharePoint Online and then decommission on-premise file servers.
☐	7.4.6 What are your customer's data security requirements and concerns?	SharePoint Online uses a group based security system with permission assignments which is very similar to most other access control implementations, for example NTFS in Windows. This will need to be well planned and implemented and decisions about delegation of permissions made.
☐	7.4.7 Which document management features should be enabled?	There are a variety of document management features available in SharePoint Online, such as versioning, approval, workflow, security, publishing and metadata creation. An organization would not usually require all these features enabled for all documents and good planning will ensure they are implemented for only those documents that would benefit from them.

☒	Question	Why this matters
☐	7.4.8 Does your customer have an intranet and if so what type of content exists on it?	SharePoint Online has many collaboration features that make it ideal for use as an intranet. Moving your customer's current intranet content is one aspect to consider but also changing their content updating processes to use SharePoint Online will need to be addressed.
☐	7.4.9 How does your customer generate and publish internal reports?	Reports and spreadsheets are typically shared internally via email. SharePoint Online can be a great place to store and highlight many company reports and statistics. You may need to consider the current processes under which such reports are built and recreate these processes within SharePoint Online, possibly using customized database lookups and workflow. SharePoint Designer is a useful tool in creating solutions such as these.
☐	7.4.10 How can I customize the SharePoint search components to best fit my customer's needs?	SharePoint Online automatically indexes content and provides a search facility, however this can be tuned to provide more accurate results if needed. You may need to evaluate the relevancy of search results over time in order to better understand if customization is needed.
☐	7.4.11 Does my customer have any business applications that would benefit from a move to SharePoint Online?	Your customer may have business applications which could be migrated or recreated in SharePoint Online using a combination of the core features, SharePoint Designer and workflow. Look to identify 'problem areas' that your customer is living with that might be a constraint of a legacy application or something that was 'knocked up' quickly but never designed for purpose and is a cause of poor user experience and/or high support overhead.

☒	Question	Why this matters
☐	7.4.12 How might SharePoint streamline my customers' business and drive productivity?	For better or worse organizations have adapted to use many ad-hoc manual and email processes to drive many aspects of their business. SharePoint Online and specifically workflow can greatly enhance the productivity of people involved in work processes. These processes may be general to HR (e.g. holiday booking) or Finance (e.g. expense reporting) or specific to support delivery of customer service. There are many possibilities and so SharePoint provides a real opportunity for a professional services engagement to find ways to improve your customers' business.
☐	7.4.13 Does your customer want a custom look and feel to SharePoint Online?	There are various templates and themes that come with SharePoint Online and more can be downloaded from Microsoft. One area that you could certainly provide support would be in the further customization of the look, feel and navigation of a SharePoint Online site typically by using SharePoint Designer
☐	7.4.14 What training needs will a SharePoint Online customer have?	Anyone who uses SharePoint Online will need some level of support and training on its day to day use. Building training modules based upon an information workers level of access is a good idea. Someone who needs to navigate and work with documents will need a different level of training than the owner of the site. You will need to perform some level of training needs analysis to determine existing and required skills.

Chapter 8

Questions about selling MS Online

There are two sides to every question

Protagoras, from Diogenes Laertius, Lives of Eminent Philosophers (Greek philosopher 485 BC - 421 BC)

THE opportunity has been revealed and you may be near to deciding what to do. At this point your thoughts will turn to the practical implications of selling and supporting MS Online and that will likely involve others.

And so in this chapter we turn to look at things that impact your planning and preparation to sell MS Online for the sales and services teams in your business.

In your organization there will be different points of view, opinion and experience to draw upon and the questions that follow will help direct those discussions.

Often it is the organizational challenges that are hardest to overcome when innovation threatens to disrupt. It can sometimes result in inertia and customer facing sales and service teams will need to be coached through the impact of online services - what it means for the business, your customers and how you compete.

8.1 Questions for sales organizations

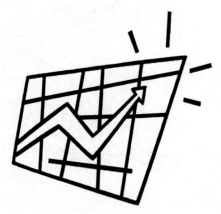

Your sales team is highly experienced and productive selling solutions that the customer installs on-premises.

Your customer understands the proposition that installs hardware and software on their premises.

And now there is MS Online.

What questions might your sales organization have in anticipation conversations with customers about MS Online?

the deal makers….the 'closers'….offer up ideas to spark conversations with customers….how to qualify interest and translate customers' needs into compelling reasons to buy….how to qualify….to sell benefits and set expectations with customers….we want satisfied customers….we have targets to meet….let's get on with it

Opportunity – the sales cry answered

Where do you start to look for opportunity?

How about customers and prospects:

- on older versions of software but challenged with justifying the cost of upgrade
- contemplating a software upgrade requiring a hardware refresh: Is there another way?
- had the shock of 'it (IT) stopped working': Is there a better way? Who can do it better?
- at the point of realization that it was the right decision 5 years ago, but not right for now; and we need it now!
- dealing with the 'IT headache' as a result of a merger or acquisition: What can we do to simplify the delivery of some common services (like email) while we focus on the knotty issues with the integration of core financial systems?
- franchise businesses looking to provide best value IT support to franchisees
- geographically dispersed places of work, those guys out in the sticks; we need to find a cost effective way to get them connected with the rest of the organization
- with a growing mobile workforce and challenged to 'keep in touch' and support them with access to data and information so they are productive

This is not an exhaustive list but even so provides plenty of clues as to where to look for opportunity.

In sales we often look for change, disruption or a compelling event as these are good indicators that the customer will be receptive, but not always.

> Change = Cloud and the availability of online services
>
> Disruption = plenty of that with the upset of a global recession
>
> Compelling event = the economy is looking up – growth is back on the agenda – let's talk business; "we need to drive productivity"

And now we look at some practical questions that are the meat of the planning and conversations with customers.

☒	Question	Why this matters
☐	8.1.1 How many of my customers have multiple locations?	Some of your customers may have already moved to a centralized IT infrastructure and others may be considering it (and you may be advising them). Keep in mind that MS Online is a centralized (hosted) IT infrastructure and may provide a cost effective alternative for your customers and in particular those that struggle with the financial justification of change.
☐	8.1.2 How many of my customers have older versions of Exchange?	The upgrade to Exchange 2007/2010 on-premise can be an expensive and time consuming process in part due to its 64 bit architecture and requirement for new server hardware. If a customer has stalled making the upgrade perhaps due to the cost then MS Online presents the opportunity to go back and discuss how you can make the upgrade affordable. See 8.1.16 for more help with this question.
☐	8.1.3 What opportunities are there around SharePoint Online?	Interest in SharePoint has increased massively over the last few years. From a customer perspective using SharePoint Online is exactly the same as using a server based deployment but priced differently. A good SharePoint site will be well designed, customized for the customer's business and integrated with Microsoft Office. You can help with all of these things and MS Online pricing may be the trigger for a customer to purchase.

☒	Question	Why this matters
☐	8.1.4 What opportunities exist with Office Communications Online?	Instant messaging is the bedfellow of email and extensively used because of its ability to see a colleague's presence status. This filters into Office and SharePoint automatically and you can customize other applications to display presence status for any contact or user. Look for opportunities to build applications and enhancements on top of the Communicator client software.
☐	8.1.5 What opportunities exist with a customer migrating to MS Online?	If your customer migrates to MS Online then you not only earn fees as PoR but have the opportunity to assist with the initial and ongoing migration of existing domain and email accounts to MS Online. This generates a consulting opportunity and leads to discussion about support for your customers' email (a business critical application for most) all providing revenue opportunities for you. See 8.2.5 also.
☐	8.1.6 How can I earn money from MS Online?	In essence the same way that you earn money already as a reseller. You earn money selling MS Online and for being a customer's ongoing PoR. You continue to provide any existing services you already offer and new professional services based upon the MS Online services acquired by your customers. You can win new customers from any location where MS Online is available (currently in 39 countries) since many of these services are location independent.

☒	Question	Why this matters
☐	8.1.7 What opportunities exist with customers acquiring Live Meeting?	Web meeting software is popular because it eliminates travel time and costs that impact productivity and cost of sales. Its use is widespread and gaining popularity. The benefit of being able to offer Live Meeting with MS Online is that you can now offer your customers a service that they may previously have been paying (someone else) much more for. Other opportunities include the sale of computer A/V equipment including the Microsoft Roundtable webcam.
☐	8.1.8 What opportunities exist for software customization?	If you have skills in software development (and even if you don't yet) you could provide customization of MS Online to better fit your customers' business needs. When you explore how products can be customized to fit the needs of your customers you are not only exploring a sales opportunity but also getting to know more about your customers' business and that often reveals more opportunity.
	8.1.9 When are MS Online individual components applicable?	Although the best pricing option is for the entire suite it is worth considering that not all customers will need all of the components. For example; some might prefer to leave email in house but use SharePoint Online or Live Meeting. MS Online is flexible to mix and match with a customer's preferred choices.

☒	Question	Why this matters
☐	8.1.10 Why MS Online rather than a free solution?	MS Online is priced aggressively but it isn't free and that means you earn money selling MS Online. Many companies use free internet software, such as Hotmail, Live Messenger or Google documents. Compare what free provides the customer and what MS Online provides and expand your customers understanding of the limitations of free. For example: Does free ensure on-going availability of the services they use? Are there limitations that inhibit customization and integration with other tools in the business? Do they have the benefit of a SLA? Accept that for some customers; free is as good as it gets. Know it; that your customers may not have considered what 'you don't get with free' so spell out for them the assurances of a SLA and the services of a PoR, see 7.2.8 for more help.
☐	8.1.11 Is there a situation where I should not propose MS Online?	MS Online was not designed with a specific customer segment or industry sector in mind. It delivers services in the Cloud for small and large enterprise customers. The Microsoft Software-plus-Services strategy accommodates a hybrid of on-premises delivery with services in the Cloud. Your value is helping your customers configure solutions that meet their needs and now you can enhance the discussion with MS Online. Don't think in terms of this or that (on-premises or MS Online). Think in terms of optimization (cost will be in this equation) and other factors (existing investments, business agility, pragmatism) that will formulate a decision path.

☒	**Question**	**Why this matters**
☐	8.1.12 Are there reasons a trial could be unsuccessful?	In some cases you and the customer might decide that after a good trial the product is not right for them. One worry however is that if you leave a customer to try things out on their own they are not going to explore the various options fully or even at all. This is an important time to focus on your customer and their buying process. You need to be involved guiding them through the various services and demonstrating their use and how you could further enhance the service with your own services. Use Live Meeting to keep in touch and keep you cost of sale low while at the same time demonstrating the power of this MS Online service. Under no circumstances leave the customer alone during the trail; develop a plan to guide them to a buying decision.
☐	8.1.13 What if my customer wants to leave MS Online?	After the renewal of the first subscription term, a customer can cancel at any time with a minimum of one-month advance notice. Upon notice, the service continues to be available for the remainder of that month and all of the following month, and charged for that period of time.
☐	8.1.14 Can a customer change the Partner of Record (PoR)?	A customer can change their PoR at any time during their subscription. This doesn't affect the initial net-add fee paid to the PoR but will affect the ongoing recurring fees paid to the PoR. Since MS Online subscription fees are fixed the only reason for a customer to change their PoR if is they feel another PoR can provide better or alternative services. This emphasizes that services are a key differentiator for those selling MS Online.

☒	Question	Why this matters
☐	8.1.15 How do I benefit by using MS Online?	Use MS Online to help you sell MS Online. Partners can get up to 250 seats (users) at no cost and keep it free if you meet sales targets in future years. That is a big incentive and helps you manage costs in your own business.
☐	8.1.16 What changes when I sell MS Online rather than a software license?	The nature of your sale with customers' changes. When selling licensed software that may involve the purchase of server hardware with professional services to bring a server into production. The customer will see this as a capital expense and usually subject that to business case/ROI review. When selling MS Online, in the same way you need to demonstrate your understanding of the business requirement and why MS Online is the best solution, but, the business case is presented differently. The cost of MS Online will be treated as a fixed term (12 months initially) operating expense. You may like to think about it as having two options to consider how you meet customers' needs whereas before you had one. In some situations, particularly if capital expenditure is tight or your customer has an urgent deadline, then you may find it easier to sell MS Online.

☒	Question	Why this matters
☐	8.1.17 Are your customers facing change or uncertainty about the future?	If they are then as you know they tend to delay making decisions. MS Online offers your customers' flexibility and that can help you close a sale. With MS Online a customer only has to predict their requirements for the next 12 months with options to upgrade (add users and others products) during the term with right to cancel at the end of the initial 12 month term (Year 1). In these challenging times customers may find this flexibility an attractive way to balance their commitments.
	8.1.18 Do I need to do anything to remind my customers to renew their subscription?	No action is necessary on your part or on the part of a customer to auto-renew. The renewed subscription maintains the same number of users, term length, billing, and payment options. A customer can also change the PO number at renewal (or at anytime) as needed. Renewal prices are determined at the time of auto-renewal. A customer can opt in or opt out of auto-renewals via MOCP at *https://mocp.microsoftonline.com/* for each individual service. Auto renew is the default option for all subscriptions unless changed by a customer.

8.2 Questions for service organizations

The nature of hosted services is the customer has outsourced and relies upon its provider(s) to deliver a service that is so often essential to the running of their business and so the performance of its provider(s) is paramount.

Earlier we presented the role of Partner of Record (PoR) and the opportunity to earn from providing managed services to your customers.

Will anything change for your services organization if you add MS Online to your portfolio?

What questions might your services organization have in anticipation of providing support for MS Online?

the friendly voice on the end of the phone when customers get into difficulty and need help....we feel good when we deliver great service and customers give positive feedback....when customers are happy with the service we provide they are receptive to ideas about other ways that we can help....service is important to maintaining customer loyalty....let's get on with it

☒	Question	Why this matters
☐	8.2.1 What is the impact on the services I provide?	MS Online does change some of the services you currently offer. Your customers' still need support for their workstations, Active Directory domain, printers, network infrastructure and other applications (some of which you will have customized). Some changes but also some new opportunities as we highlight later. MS Online does offer an alternative style of delivery to some existing services (such as email) but also offers services that are not currently used and present new opportunities for you to offer professional services.
☐	8.2.2 What changes with Exchange when delivered with MS Online?	The maintenance and backup of Exchange is handled automatically. Your customers will still need support with adds, deletes and changes to email addresses, groups, contacts and to configure SPAM filters.
☐	8.2.3 Do I lose the support of mail servers when a customer chooses MS Online?	If the customer migrates all email to MS Online then this a fundamental question for you and possibly one of the biggest changes to your business. Does the fact that you no longer need to support mail to the same degree mean that you are free to focus on higher value consultancy and professional services or does it prejudice a significant part of your existing revenue stream?
☐	8.2.4 What opportunities exist with Office Communications Online?	Instant messaging is the bedfellow of email and extensively used because of its ability to see colleagues presence status. This filters into Office and SharePoint automatically and you can customize other applications to display presence status for any contact or user. You can also build applications and enhancements on top of the Communicator client software.

☒	Question	Why this matters
☐	8.2.5 What opportunities exist with a customer migrating to MS Online?	Many customers will need assistance with the initial and ongoing migration of existing domain and email accounts to MS Online. Domain user accounts will need to be kept synchronized. Mail will need to be moved, forwarded and maybe redirected. Workstations will need to be reconfigured. You may need to do exports from other online services. Microsoft have provided tools and documentation to assist with these tasks but they are aimed at those who are technically savvy – i.e. you
☐	8.2.6 What training opportunities exist with MS Online?	Look for customers that have little or no experience with SharePoint, Live Meeting for sending instant messages and using presence. They could benefit greatly with training on how to use SharePoint effectively, how to host and attend Live Meetings and make best use of presence. You should evaluate with your customer aspects of MS Online administration they prefer to control and where they need you to provide training and a 2nd line support desk.

☒	Question	Why this matters
☐	8.2.7 What opportunities exist for software customization?	If you have skills in software development (and even if you don't yet) you could provide customization of MS Online to better fit your customers' business needs. You can access Exchange web services and enhance the Communicator client software but by far the biggest scope for customization is SharePoint. By creating forms and custom workflows using SharePoint Designer you can create web based versions of the applications and business processes that your customers have. You don't need to be a developer to do this – grab yourself a book on SharePoint Designer and start earning from customizing SharePoint.
☐	8.2.8 Are there any add on services I should offer for free?	No. One benefit of software customization is the ability of re-use at little incremental cost to you. Particularly when it comes to SharePoint customizations you will need to decide how much to provide at no or a low cost to persuade the customer to sign up with you and how much to charge extra for.

☒	Question	Why this matters
☐	8.2.9 How is my customers' data managed by MS Online?	All MS Online services are highly available and backed up to meet the SLA. Other than Outlook deleted item recovery and the SharePoint recycle bin you have no direct access to lost emails and files. If you need to provide full individual item recovery to some or all users then those accounts should be kept on-premise or consider client side archiving or backup. For email and IM consider Exchange Hosted Archiving. MS Online fully supports coexistence scenarios where some users and services are in MS Online and others are not. You need to know these options to appropriately advise your customer based on their policies and operational needs.
☐	8.2.10 What if my customer wants to leave MS Online?	A new customer signs up for an initial 12 month subscription. They have the option to cancel within the first 30 days of their initial subscription (they will be charged one month's subscription). After the first 30 days they are committed to the balance of the initial subscription (11 months). After the first subscription term of 12 months a customer may cancel by giving 30 days notice. This might apply where a customer wishes to migrate to an on-premises installation of software. There are migration tools supplied (command line only) for a move back to on-premise or to another provider you may determine there is an opportunity to offer paid for support and professional services to enable migration.

☒	Question	Why this matters
☐	8.2.11 Will MS Online change any aspects of how we deliver services?	MS Online supports office-based (location based), deskless (no fixed location and restricted time access to a network) and mobile workers (work from anywhere and hop on and off networks). If you are accustomed to supporting these types of users then no change really. MS Online is available in 39 countries across multiple time zones so do check with your customers where their users are geographically located and agree access to and availability of your services. This may signal a need to develop a partnership with other MS Online partners that have the same customer situation.
☐	8.2.12 How will my negotiated SLA with my customers be affected?	Microsoft offers a SLA for MS Online. You may have your own negotiated SLA with customers for support/services that you provide. Where you are the PoR for a MS Online customer you need to consider how MS Online affects your ability to meet your SLA and support your customer, e.g. workstations, recover deleted user data and accounts.

Funny you should say that

To acquire knowledge, one must study; but to acquire wisdom, one must observe.

Marilyn vos Savant (author, lecturer, playwright and listed in Guinness Book of Records under "Highest IQ")

THE engine of the Cloud is the Internet that has 1.8 billion users and is growing. Examples of the Cloud are everywhere in the home and business and here we recount stories that might just help reconcile your thoughts.

I'm sure that you have your own stories – so let us know them: *stories@Smart-Questions.com*

Business is personal

The MD of a small ISV had made the decision to move the business to SaaS. It was their calculated bet that this was the future for their business and being a risk all strategy they had to get the sales team on board. Despite their efforts the sales team did not 'get it' and that led to the painful decision to let the sales team go and re-hire. The future can be a scary place and some people prefer the security of the present day. It's also a people question.

If it ain't broke don't fix it

But when it does break do you fix it or change it?

A small consulting firm had their email server hacked and it did not come to the attention of the owner until they noticed they were not receiving email. Hiring in someone to fix it was going to be expensive and take a few days to arrange to bring the server back to life.

This was one occasion to ask the question: how do I prevent this ever happening again?

The resulting questions that arise: who can do it, do it better, do it cheaper and prevent it ever happening again?

BPOS would be a solution for this firm.

Try before you Buy

This has become popular and made easy with the Cloud. Like many others you have probably downloaded software with no certain intention of buying but out of curiosity. You try it and let the trial expire and sometimes you buy.

The one thing that influences a buying decision is contact made with the customer during the trial. If you offer try before you buy then make sure your customer's experience includes personal contact and have something useful to say other than: "your trial ends in 7 days do you want to buy now?"

Developing this rapport will be essential for customer service teams to drive try to buy conversions.

Keeping up with change

Compare 10 years ago when you were shopping to buy a new television and how you would approach that same purchase today.

Compare 5 years ago when you were shopping for a short-break holiday and how you would approach that today.

Today customers looking to acquire online services have a high propensity to search online. To capture these customers make sure your online assets are easily found. Most importantly make it easy for your customer to move from being online to speaking to someone who is knowledgeable and with great customer service skills in your business.

Do what you do best and leave the rest to others

One of the big decisions faced by those that want to deliver services in the Cloud is: do I host the services, should I use the hosting services of a reputable hosting provider or sell the services offered by a market leading company like Microsoft?

Do Delta build the aircraft that they fly? No, delivering a comfortable and safe travel experience is their forte not building aeroplanes.

Apply this same test to your business. Also consider how your customers would apply the test in their businesses.

Need and Want, Core and Context

In our personal lives we often determine our priorities by what we 'need' as against what we 'want' and can afford. In business the same tests apply. Take for example how email would be prioritized.

Does the business need or rely upon email? It is hard in truth to answer No to this question. So, the answer is Yes.

Is email core (vital) to the business? Most will answer Yes.

Are you an email business? No.

Ah-ha! Then email is core to the business but you are not an email business. So email as a service to the business is context.

The test you might choose to apply for context is: who can do it, do it better, and do it cheaper? In other words; what is the best economic solution available to the business? For some that may translate as; what can we afford?

"Busy come back later" finds you new customers

The guys in IT are hard pushed and sometimes Line of Business (LoB) managers get the "we are busy, come back later" from them. Meantime the LoB manager has a business to run and in truth who reacts favorably to busy come back later?

Vendors offering services in the Cloud provide an attractive combination of try before you buy, no IT involvement, rapid deployment and use of your own departmental budget. The IT estate of businesses is changing. IT won't always have the last word and that is liberating for LoB managers.

The politics of selling to organizations is changing so will you continue to stand behind IT or also open doors to meet with the LoB managers?

Keep in mind that in big business this is likely to change over time as CIOs and IT managers rein in the expanding real estate of IT with addition (sometimes ad-hoc) of online services.

When selling to SMBs getting the attention of decision makers is a challenge and they might only have capacity for one IT initiative a year. Make sure your have the compelling proposition. Earlier in the book we talked about how to break into SMB's with research that links the adoption of hosted services to financial performance. Go get 'em.

Past performance is no predictor of the future

In most IT businesses you will have experienced ups and downs and forecasting is notoriously hazardous.

One of the things about subscription based services is the predictability about future revenue. There is never any cast iron guarantee but retention rates of 95% are being experienced and that is a lot more interesting than the binary 'you win – you lose' of licensed software deals.

It does take time to build the subscription revenue associated with online services but it is cumulative and that is a bit like compound interest.

Who is interested? Owners of businesses who are looking to build the valuation of their business are. The VC community is particularly active in searching out companies in the Cloud and is determining valuations of 5x annual revenues for established businesses.

If IT is a utility, what is utility service?

If IT is a utility that is switched on by your provider and they bill you for usage then what is service in this utility world?

The base assumption for a utility is that it works and it is rare that it is unavailable – but when it is you quickly need it restored.

So, does service become something that jumps into action when things go wrong? Yes. That becomes quite challenging for providers with utility sized numbers of customers all affected at the same time.

Service in a utility world becomes a focus for prevention and avoidance of events that affect customers and thus having to say sorry and financially compensate customers.

When you partner for the delivery of IT as a utility to your customers – choose carefully.

Less is More

The IT industry is a hot bed of research and development that will continue to innovate and amaze. We have a huge appetite for innovation yet in our lives we don't have so much time to get our heads around this stuff.

Our ability to absorb innovation will be a factor of how much time it takes to become proficient and deliver productivity gains. Removing the need to install and maintain software is all part of that equation.

It appears this is where the Cloud is headed – less is more – and will fuel growth for vendors of online services in the Cloud and, lest we forget, productivity for customers.

Trends

Technology pundits are writing with a cross-over of technology with economic analysis and this has come to a head with the global recession. Analysis of the economics of 'own and operate' versus the Cloud are debated but wise heads also know that there are other business fundamentals of note.

What lessons have been learned from the recession?

How quickly were businesses able to react to change?

The questions of 'agility' and 'pragmatism' come to mind. When thinking about the approaches you might take when advising your customer on their next IT project or IT refresh take the conversation in the direction of how agility and pragmatism both from a technology and financial perspective plays to your purpose (to close the sale) and your customer's benefit (making decisions in an uncertain world).

Growth is back on the agenda

With the advent of online services comes the opportunity to offer a 'managed service' to the customer and while this is nothing new it provides incremental and new revenue opportunities to grow your business.

In a recent report by MSPmentor[35] they surveyed the top 100 Managed Service Providers (per their industry survey) and reported that the top 25% posted >50% year on year growth 2009 vs. 2008.

Crystal ball not needed

In a recent Gartner briefing attended by the author their public view is that the Cloud is "beyond a bubble"[36]. What does that mean for your business and for your customers' businesses? In reality that is what everyone is trying to figure and one of the ways to do that is to partner with Microsoft who is in a powerful position to set the agenda with customers.

---

[35] MSPmentor the voice of managed service providers at www.mspmentor.net

[36] Gartner briefing 10/09/2009 on the Cloud led by Mike Spink Research Director.

Be the conversation leader

The IT industry has a lot of jargon and while we use it as a vocabulary most of our customers do not, just as we struggle to learn their vocabulary.

Confused customers do not buy what they don't understand any more than you should buy stock in a business you do not understand.

In particular, as much as we like the word 'Cloud' it is not a meaningful word for customers. What exactly does it describe?

To be a conversation leader here is a quick resume to practice how you can describe (in your own words) a customer conversation.

Customer: *So what's going on in the big bad world of IT? I read all sorts of new developments with software and something called the Cloud.*

You: *The IT industry is in its sixth decade and you would not recognize it from its beginnings. Today it connects the world and has a major impact on how we work, learn and socialize. It makes life more interesting and the economic benefits are evident. What I'm interested in is to understand how these new developments that you speak can help your business. What is the single biggest challenge for you as a business to harness IT for your benefit?*

You could have responded with: Ah the Cloud, yes it's great, Software as a Service provides a new way for customers to rent software. Did you know Microsoft has a huge online business and a new product called MS Online – it works in the Cloud – and available to buy now.....

We hope the point is made. This is not about technology, something else; something big no doubt, is already being worked on in a skunkworks project somewhere in the world that will prove disruptive in 10 years time.

It is about progress and how we benefit from progress. How we describe that can make a huge difference to whether people get it or ignore it – they need it put in terms they understand – you need to do that - so it is back to selling basics.

Funny you should say that

Chapter

Case Studies – People Like You

The reality is that changes are coming... They must come. You must share in bringing them.

John Hersey (American writer, 1914 - 1993)

WE have provided many questions and you may already have the answers to some of those questions. Now you are probably interested to hear from your peers, other people with hopes, fears and ambitions who also faced a raft of questions.

Rather than highlight a few case studies here we signpost you to Microsoft's case studies web site where you can search on case studies that you deem most relevant and interesting to you.

This is a great resource and you access it by following this link:

http://www.microsoft.com/casestudies/Case_Study_Search_Results.aspx?Type=1&ProTaxID=3278,15244

Chapter

11

A new day, a new way

Everything you can imagine is real.

Pablo Picasso *(Spanish Cubist painter, 1881 - 1973)*

THIS is a fictional story to bring to life the potential of change as it is described in this book. Change can be disruptive and unpredictable. Change is opportunity – for some.

The story is about a small business start-up (LeanCo) in San Francisco describing its inception then later how the business grows, prospers and is then acquired.

The owners of LeanCo are ambitious and while they know about IT they rely on others to advise them what to specify and buy for the business. There is no money to employ IT staff at this time and this is typical in a start-up business where the focus is on providing basic IT support at a low cost while carefully managing cash flow.

The primary focus for the business is sales and IT must support the people that will win the business that will make or break the company. Anyone that has bootstrapped a business will recognize this situation and know the challenges.

The first priority of a new business is to let its customers know they are open for business so the first thing they do is to establish ways to promote the business and make contact with customers.

As a priority LeanCo decide they urgently need:

- A web site

- email and mobile email

- A basic accounting package

With no money coming in they are using their start-up funds and they prioritize that money to spend on outbound marketing.

As a small business LeanCo employees work from home and sometimes from a serviced office – they do not have dedicated desks (they are deskless) and rely heavily upon access to the Internet (fixed and mobile) and use of mobile phones. They visit clients and need to be able to work both offline and online.

The outbound marketing and web site is generating enquiries and to both their surprise and delight enquiries are coming in from all over the country.

That presents a challenge as going to visit these customers will put a strain on the people resources and cash available. They need to qualify the interest of these customers (actually little more than suspects at this time) and to do it in a professional way without the time and cost of travelling to each customer. They need a solution now otherwise the enquiries will go cold.

As a priority and within hours they need:

- A way to present their company, products and service online

The web meetings go well and a number of customers are now confirmed prospects and keeping records of prospects in a spreadsheet is problematic. Two follow ups with customers are missed and notes about contacts with prospects are not available to everyone. This comes to a head when the VP of a prospect calls and the VP dealing with the sale is on vacation in England and not easily contactable.

They need:

> • A way to record all information about sales, prospects and customers

The business is busy producing product data sheets, price lists, customer proposals, and commercial documents distributed by email so everyone has a copy. Document templates are created and again are distributed by email to everyone. Everyone is busy and documents are frequently revised and version control is a problem with the current method of distributing documents by email.

When the wrong version of a proposal template is used and sent to a prospect the business recognizes a problem.

They need:

> • A way to share documents that is highly accessible yet secure

Customers like the product and more people in customer organizations are making contact with LeanCo. Many of the requests for information are similar and while LeanCo love the opportunity to speak to customers it is time consuming to handle some requests that come from people who are not a decision/budget authority. The web site is too public to use for some information that they prefer to make available only to customers and besides it creates a community feel.

They need:

> • A way to create a portal for customers with shared and dedicated partitions

LeanCo expand their product range and customers are now repeat ordering and sales order processing costs are starting to escalate and impact margins. Order volumes are growing and response times that customers are accustomed to being kept are but only by extra hours put in by staff. This is great news but the Sales Order Processing (SOP) team is stressed and some staff leave. LeanCo found it easy to re-hire but training staff is draining productivity of experienced staff. Customers tell how other suppliers provide online ordering and how convenient they find that. LeanCo also realize they would benefit by automating some of its SOP processes.

They need:

> • A way for customers to browse and purchase online with orders
>   automatically routed to SOP workflow

LeanCo is now an established business with a trading history to
compete for larger contracts. They start contacting large customers
to find out about how to become a supplier. These customers are
highly organized with supplier portals and stipulate the use of
eCommerce that requires suppliers to be able to transact business
electronically (paperless trading) for the order to pay cycle.

They need:

> • A way to send and receive electronic documents (orders, invoices)
>   preferably integrated to SOP and Invoicing functions

The basic accounting system can no longer cope. A decision is
made to upgrade to an ERP system but the cost is frightening and
the implementation time will take them into the next fiscal year and
they really want to upgrade ahead of that time. Part of the issue is
that LeanCo still has no dedicated IT staff and are reliant upon
ERP vendors and consultants and they are expensive people to
hire. It can't wait and they need a solution that they can afford.
The ERP hardware and software costs are going to have a major
impact on working capital. It is a worrying time.

They need:

> • A way to implement ERP without major capital cost and do it quickly

As LeanCo win business with large customers sales transactions
turn into projects and that requires record keeping for time and
expenses as some costs are internal and some are invoiced to the
customer. LeanCo is concerned that no system exists and this is a
black hole to lose money in.

They need:

> • A way to organize and run projects and keep time keeping records and
>   record allocation of expenses to projects

The business has grown fast and at the current rate of growth will
soon have 100 employees. One employee asked for a copy of their
signed Contract of Employment as their copy had been destroyed

in a house fire. They found it, eventually, after a long search. They have a range of benefits for employees but not all employees have the same benefits and they need to compile these records but it will be difficult and so keep putting it off. Holiday requests and records are a mess and they are not sure what remaining holiday entitlement some employees have.

The current arrangements for employee reviews are chaotic and some employees do not have recorded performance targets and objectives. They know they have to do better; their employees are an asset to the business.

They need:

- **An HR system that is accessible to all employees**

Business is good and LeanCo is recognized as a successful business and attracts the interest of competitors. It is profitable and has attracted some bid interest. Finally a too good to be true offer is made and LeanCo goes under due diligence by the bidder. Part of the due diligence involves a review of IT and existing IT staff comprising one person carrying the title, Manager – IT Resources, who is responsible for managing the relationship with IT vendors. He is a Microsoft Certified Professional but does very little hands on - that is all outsourced.

The bidder remarks that LeanCo's IT assets are small for a business of its size and that the running cost to the business for IT is low. It also remarks how well developed IT is for a business of it size and years of trading. In fact it attributes this to why they are achieving above average margins.

Now the bidder negotiates hard on price but LeanCo stand firm; they have a good business and the foundations for growth. The bidder is secretly impressed with what they have achieved with IT and how that as a model would transform its own business. It sees wisdom in LeanCo's decision to use the Cloud as this means there is no legacy IT systems and associated costs in the business to absorb creating a liability to them as the acquiring organization.

The deal is done and later in a celebration two employees are talking about their idea for a business and how what they had learned at LeanCo about the Cloud would be ideal for their new business venture.

And the point of the story is?

While this is a fictitious story every aspect of IT described in this story is available today in the Cloud.

You, and perhaps more importantly your customers, have the opportunity to be part of it. Make sure they go there with you.

Chapter

Final Word

I have always thought the actions of men the best interpreters of their thoughts.

John Locke (English empiricist philosopher 1632 - 1704)

AND so to the point of this book; do you think you are about to witness a fundamental shift in how your customers use software?

The book asks the big question: Thinking of…selling Microsoft Online Services?

Particularly it poses the question and helps you know the answer to; should I be selling Microsoft MS Online?

We have sought to stimulate your interest so you can make your decision.

You have the final word.

Appendix - Online Resources

Microsoft has a number of online resources available for partners to access. Access to some online resources will require you are a member of the Microsoft Partner Network:

https://partner.microsoft.com

https://partner.microsoft.com/partnerprofit

Enrol as a Microsoft Advisor at:

https://www.quickstartonlineservices.com

Administration Centre at:

https://admin.microsoftonline.com

Microsoft Online Services Customer Portal at:

https://mocp.microsoftonline.com/site/default.aspx

Microsoft Licensing and Business Policy Guide to download at:

http://www.microsoft.com/online/buy.mspx#guide

Microsoft Business Productivity Online Suite training -
https://www.microsoft.com.au/events/register/home.aspx?levent=611380&l invitation

Microsoft Business Productivity Online Suite Migration training -
https://training.partner.microsoft.com/learning/app/management/LMS_Ac tDetails.aspx?UserMode=0&ActivityId=577446

Microsoft Provisioning Guide -
https://www.quickstartonlineservices.com/partner/Readiness%20Documents /Business%20Productivity%20Online%20Standard%20Suite%20Provisioni ng%20Guide.zip

All URLs correct at time of publication (June 2010).

Notes pages

Thank you for purchasing this book we hope it has been a source of inspiration and provide below a place for all the ideas and questions that occurred to you on your reading journey.

Notes pages